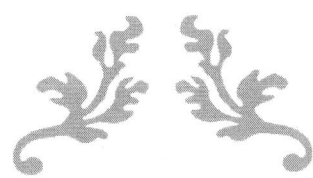

VILNIUS TRAVEL GUIDE 2024

A Christmas Vacation Full Of Charm And Tradition

EDWIN P. WILLIAMS

All Right Reserved

No part of this book may be produced, stored in a retrieval system, or transmitted in any form or by any means, electronic or mechanical, photocopying, recording or otherwise, without the prior written permission of the copyright owner

Copyright Edwin P. Williams

Disclaimer

The world is constantly changing. Hotels change ownership or close, restaurants might adjust their prices, museums could alter their closing hours, and transportation routes can be modified. These changes can happen even after our authors have visited, inspected and written about these places

While we strive to keep all information as current as possible, some changes may inevitable occur before a new edition of this guidebook is published.

Thank you for choosing our guidebook, we hope you have a wonderful trip.

Introduction to Vilnius at Christmas 3

Getting to Vilnius 9

Where to Stay in Vilnius During Christmas 17

Vilnius Christmas Markets 27

Top Christmas Attractions in Vilnius 37

Vilnius Christmas Train: A Festive Ride Around the City 53

Shopping for Christmas in Vilnius 63

Winter Activities and Outdoor Adventures 77

Religious and Cultural Traditions 84

Family-Friendly Christmas Experiences 89

New Year's Eve in Vilnius 99

Practical Information 104

Conclusion: Why Vilnius Is the Perfect Christmas Destination 110

Vilnius Sample Itinerary: A Magical Christmas Experience .. 114

Introduction to Vilnius at Christmas

As an experienced travel writer with a passion for uncovering the hidden gems of lesser-known destinations, I have had the privilege of exploring some of Europe's most charming cities, but there is something truly magical about Vilnius during Christmas. situated in the heart of Lithuania, this city is a breathtaking blend of old-world charm, deep-rooted traditions, and a festive spirit that captivates anyone who visits during the holiday season.

My first visit to Vilnius was several years ago, and it didn't take long for me to fall in love with its enchanting streets, where history and modernity coexist in perfect harmony. I've traveled here multiple times, but there's something about Vilnius in December that makes it even more special. Imagine strolling through the cobblestone streets of the Old Town, illuminated by thousands of twinkling lights, with the scent of mulled wine and cinnamon pastries filling the air. The towering Christmas tree in Cathedral Square, always designed with a creative twist, is a sight that rivals even the grandest displays across Europe.

What sets Vilnius apart is its authentic, uncommercialized Christmas experience.

You won't find overwhelming crowds, but you will find warmth, both in the city's welcoming locals and the cozy cafés that beckon you to escape the winter chill. I have gathered every essential detail to guide you through the city's Christmas markets, where traditional Lithuanian crafts and foods create the perfect holiday gifts. I'll take you on a journey through the best local restaurants where you can indulge in hearty Christmas dishes, and I'll show you the best spots to explore Vilnius' winter wonderland, from ice-skating rinks to snow-covered castles.

In this book, you will find not only practical advice, but also my personal recommendations for making the most of your time in Vilnius during Christmas. Whether it's your first visit or you're returning to rediscover the city, this guide is designed to be your trusted companion. I have distilled my experiences, insider tips, and passion for this beautiful city into one comprehensive resource. If you're seeking a unique, authentic, and memorable Christmas vacation, this guide is for you. Let's explore Vilnius together, and I guarantee you will fall in love with its festive charm, just as I did.

Overview of Vilnius

Vilnius, the capital of Lithuania, is a city steeped in history, culture, and architectural beauty. Known for its remarkably preserved Baroque Old Town, a UNESCO World Heritage site, Vilnius seamlessly combines its rich past with a vibrant, modern energy.

Winding cobblestone streets lead to charming squares, historic churches, and grand palaces, while trendy cafes, boutiques, and art galleries add a contemporary flair to the city's timeless appeal.

Vilnius is often referred to as one of Europe's hidden gems, a city that has managed to maintain its authenticity while offering a wide array of experiences for travelers. From exploring the hilltop Gediminas Tower with panoramic views over the city to wandering through Užupis, the bohemian district with its own independent "republic," Vilnius offers a blend of tradition and creativity that surprises and delights visitors.

What truly sets Vilnius apart is its welcoming and friendly atmosphere. Lithuanians take pride in their heritage, and this warmth extends to travelers who come to discover their capital city. During Christmas, Vilnius transforms into an even more magical destination, with a festive charm that is both intimate and grand.

What Makes Vilnius Special During Christmas

Vilnius during Christmas is like stepping into a fairytale. The city lights up with festive decorations, twinkling lights, and an enormous, creatively designed Christmas tree that becomes the centerpiece of Cathedral Square. The markets come alive with the sounds of Christmas carols, the smell of traditional holiday foods, and the warmth of mulled wine stalls.

What makes Vilnius so special during this time is the authenticity of its celebrations. Unlike the often-commercialized Christmas events in larger European capitals, Vilnius offers a more intimate, community-focused experience. The Christmas markets are a place where locals and visitors mingle, sharing in the joy of the season with traditional Lithuanian crafts, food, and music. Whether you're ice skating in the city center or taking a festive train ride through the twinkling streets, there is an undeniable sense of magic in the air.

Vilnius also embraces its spiritual and religious traditions during Christmas. Midnight mass at the Cathedral Basilica of St. Stanislaus and St. Ladislaus is a revered event, and the city's churches host concerts and services that reflect the true meaning of the holiday.

Historical and Cultural Significance of Christmas in Vilnius

Christmas in Vilnius is deeply rooted in both religious and cultural traditions. As a predominantly Catholic country, Lithuania observes Christmas with a blend of Christian customs and pagan winter solstice rituals. The Christmas Eve dinner, known as Kūčios, is the most significant part of the holiday. It is a time when families gather for a meal consisting of 12 traditional dishes, none of which include meat. Each dish symbolizes the 12 apostles, and the meal is prepared with great care and respect for tradition. From dishes like herring in various forms to kūčiukai (small, crunchy pastries served with poppy seed milk), Kūčios represents the importance of family, reflection, and gratitude.

Another unique aspect of the Lithuanian Christmas tradition is the practice of caroling. Groups of carolers, often children, go door to door singing traditional songs, spreading cheer, and receiving small treats in return. This custom reinforces the sense of community and hospitality that defines the Lithuanian Christmas season.

Historically, Vilnius has also been a center of diverse cultural influences, from Polish and Jewish to Russian and German. These influences have shaped how the city celebrates Christmas, infusing the holiday with a mix of traditions that reflect Vilnius' multicultural past.

Weather and Climate in December

December in Vilnius marks the arrival of winter, and the weather is often cold but beautiful, with temperatures ranging from around -2°C to -8°C (28°F to 17°F). Snowfall is common, covering the city in a picturesque white blanket that enhances the festive atmosphere. The short daylight hours (approximately 6 to 7 hours of daylight) add to the coziness of the season, with early sunsets allowing the city's Christmas lights and decorations to shine brightly in the long winter evenings.

For travelers, it's important to dress warmly, as Vilnius' winter can be biting, especially with the wind. Layered clothing, warm boots, hats, scarves, and gloves are essential for enjoying the outdoor Christmas markets, ice skating, and the scenic winter walks through the Old Town.

However, the cold weather also makes it the perfect time to warm up in one of Vilnius' many cozy cafes, where you can enjoy hot chocolate or mulled wine while watching the snow fall outside.

Despite the chilly temperatures, the holiday season in Vilnius is nothing short of enchanting. The snow, the lights, and the festive spirit come together to create an unforgettable Christmas experience in a city that feels both welcoming and magical.

1

Getting to Vilnius

Vilnius, as the capital of Lithuania, is well connected by air, rail, bus, and car, making it relatively easy to reach, whether you're arriving from nearby European countries or from farther afield. For travelers visiting during the Christmas season, Vilnius offers a smooth and efficient journey into its magical winter landscape, with transport options that cater to every need. Here's everything you need to know about how to get to Vilnius for your Christmas vacation.

a) By Air: Vilnius International Airport (VNO)

Vilnius International Airport (VNO) is the largest and most important airport in Lithuania, handling the majority of the country's air traffic. Located approximately 6 kilometers (3.7 miles) south of the city center, the airport is well-organized and traveler-friendly, offering modern facilities and efficient services. The address for Vilnius International Airport is Rodūnios kl. 10A, Vilnius 02189, Lithuania.

The airport is a hub for international and domestic flights, connecting Vilnius with major European cities and beyond. VNO has one terminal that handles both arrivals and departures, making navigation straightforward for travelers. During the Christmas season, the airport is adorned with festive decorations, welcoming passengers with the warmth of the holiday spirit.

Major Airlines and Flight Routes

Vilnius International Airport is served by a variety of international airlines, offering both direct and connecting flights to numerous destinations across Europe. Some of the major airlines that operate at VNO include:

Ryanair: Offering budget-friendly flights from cities like London, Dublin, and Berlin.

Wizz Air: Providing affordable connections to locations such as Warsaw, Vienna, and Milan.

airBaltic: Connecting Vilnius with cities like Riga, Tallinn, and other Baltic and European destinations.

LOT Polish Airlines: Offering flights from Warsaw and other key European hubs.

Lufthansa: Connecting Vilnius with Frankfurt and Munich, providing access to international flights worldwide.

There are direct flights to and from key European cities such as London, Paris, Berlin, Vienna, Copenhagen, and Amsterdam, making Vilnius accessible from most major European capitals within 2-3 hours.

For travelers from the United States, Asia, or other continents, you will likely have to connect via a major European hub such as Frankfurt, Munich, Warsaw, or Copenhagen.

Airport Transfers: Taxis, Ride-Sharing, Public Transport

Once you arrive at Vilnius International Airport, you have several options to reach the city center:

1. Taxis

Taxis are readily available outside the arrivals terminal. A taxi ride to the city center takes about 15-20 minutes, depending on traffic, and costs between €10 to €15. It's recommended to use official taxi services or ride-sharing apps like Bolt to avoid overcharging. Taxi services are reliable, and many drivers speak English, making it a convenient option for travelers.

2. Ride-Sharing

Ride-sharing services such as Bolt and Uber are also available at Vilnius International Airport. Ride-share fares to the city center typically range from €7 to €12, depending on demand and the time of day. Like taxis, these services take approximately 15-20 minutes to reach the city center.

3. Public Transport: Bus

Vilnius is known for its efficient public transport system. Bus route 88 and 3G provide direct connections between the airport and the city center. Buses run frequently (every 10-15 minutes), and the journey takes about 20-25 minutes, with a fare of €1 for a single ride (or €0.65 with an e-ticket).

4. Train

The airport has a small train station located a short walk from the terminal. Trains to Vilnius Central Station run every 30-40 minutes and take about 7 minutes to reach the city center. The fare is €0.70, making this the fastest and most economical option for solo travelers with light luggage. The train station in Vilnius is centrally located, giving easy access to the Old Town and most hotels.

b) By Train: Rail Connections from Neighboring Countries

Vilnius is connected by rail to several major cities in neighboring countries, although train connections from Western Europe are somewhat limited. The central railway station, Vilnius Train Station (Geležinkelio Stotis), is located just south of the Old Town, making it convenient for visitors.

Travelers can take advantage of the following international routes:

Warsaw to Vilnius: A comfortable overnight train journey via Kaunas with transfers is available, making Poland a popular gateway for travelers from Central Europe.

Riga to Vilnius: Buses are more common, but there are occasional rail connections that pass through the scenic Baltic countryside.

Minsk to Vilnius: A direct train route links Minsk, Belarus, with Vilnius, offering a short 2-hour journey for those visiting from Eastern Europe.

Train services are generally affordable, but schedules should be checked in advance, particularly during the winter months when timetables may be adjusted.

c) By Bus: International and Domestic Bus Services

For travelers preferring buses, Vilnius is well-connected to neighboring countries through a variety of international bus services. Buses are often a cheaper alternative to trains, with multiple daily services to cities like Warsaw, Riga, Tallinn, and Minsk.

Lux Express and **Ecolines** are the major international bus operators, providing comfortable long-distance travel with amenities such as Wi-Fi, air conditioning, and reclining seats.

Travel times:

Warsaw to Vilnius: Approximately 8-9 hours.

Riga to Vilnius: Around 4-5 hours.

Tallinn to Vilnius: About 8-9 hours.

Domestic bus services connect Vilnius to other Lithuanian cities, including Kaunas, Klaipėda, and Trakai, making it easy to explore the rest of the country.

d) By Car: Road Trip Routes and Tips

Driving to Vilnius is an excellent option for those who enjoy road trips.

The city is connected by a well-maintained network of highways. Whether you're driving in from Poland, Latvia, or Belarus, the journey offers scenic views of the Baltic landscape.

Warsaw to Vilnius: The drive takes approximately 6-7 hours, with border crossings between Poland and Lithuania usually being smooth.

Riga to Vilnius: Around 4-5 hours on the A2 and E67 highways.

If you plan to drive during the winter, be prepared for potentially snowy conditions. Lithuanian highways are well-maintained, but it's essential to have winter tires and ensure your car is equipped for winter driving. Parking in Vilnius is relatively easy, with paid parking lots and garages available near the Old Town and most tourist attractions.

e) **Local Transportation: Public Transit, Taxis, and Rental Cars**

Once in Vilnius, the city's public transportation network is efficient and affordable. The system consists of buses and trolleybuses, with an extensive network covering all parts of the city. A single journey costs €1 (or €0.65 with an e-ticket), and 24-hour passes are available for around €5. Public transit is a great way to explore Vilnius during your stay, especially for short distances.

Taxis and Ride-Sharing: Taxis and services like Bolt and Uber are widely available and affordable, making them a good option for getting around, particularly in colder weather.

Rental Cars: If you prefer the freedom of driving, several international car rental companies operate from Vilnius International Airport and the city center. Rental prices start around €20-30 per day, depending on the vehicle type and insurance.

No matter how you choose to arrive, Vilnius welcomes you with open arms, offering a mix of modern convenience and old-world charm that makes getting to and around the city easy and enjoyable.

2

Where to Stay in Vilnius During Christmas

As the festive season draws in and the city of Vilnius transforms into a winter wonderland, choosing the right accommodation can make all the difference in your Christmas vacation. Whether you're looking for five-star luxury, cozy mid-range comfort, or budget-friendly stays, Vilnius offers an array of lodging options that cater to every type of traveler. Below is a comprehensive guide to the best accommodations during Christmas, including luxury hotels, budget stays, and unique boutique options that make the holiday season extra special.

Luxury Hotels: Top 5-Star Options

For those seeking a lavish Christmas retreat, Vilnius has some excellent luxury hotels that combine historic elegance with modern comfort.

1. Kempinski Hotel Cathedral Square

Address: Universiteto g. 14, Vilnius 01122

Price Range: €250-€400 per night

Contact: +370 5 220 1160 | reservations.vilnius@kempinski.com

Description: Overlooking Cathedral Square, the Kempinski is one of the most prestigious hotels in Vilnius. Its grand, elegant rooms offer breathtaking views of the Christmas tree and Vilnius' Old Town. The hotel features an indoor swimming pool, a luxurious spa, and a gourmet restaurant.

During the holiday season, the Kempinski often has a special Christmas package, including a festive dinner. Major attractions like Gediminas Tower and the Palace of the Grand Dukes are just steps away.

2. Hotel Pacai

Address: Didžioji g. 7, Vilnius 01128

Price Range: €230-€350 per night

Contact: +370 5 277 4200 | info@hotelpacai.com

Description: Housed in a 17th-century mansion, Hotel Pacai combines historical Baroque elegance with contemporary luxury. The rooms are sophisticated and spacious, and guests can enjoy the hotel's fine dining restaurant, spa, and wellness center. Located in the heart of Vilnius Old Town, it's an ideal base for exploring the city's Christmas markets and historical sites, such as the Gates of Dawn and Vilnius University.

3. Radisson Blu Royal Astorija

Address: Didžioji g. 35/2, Vilnius 01128

Price Range: €180-€280 per night

Contact: +370 5 212 0110 | info.astorija.vilnius@radissonblu.com

Description: The Radisson Blu Royal Astorija Hotel is located in the vibrant Old Town and offers stunning views of the city.

With its classic architecture and modern amenities, the hotel includes a fitness center, indoor pool, and fine dining at Brasserie Astorija. Guests are a short walk away from Vilnius' Christmas festivities, including the Christmas markets and Bernardine Gardens.

4. Narutis Hotel

Address: Pilies g. 24, Vilnius 01123

Price Range: €160-€250 per night

Contact: +370 5 212 2894 | reservations@narutis.com

Description: This historic five-star hotel offers a rich sense of history with modern luxury. Each room is unique, combining original period features with modern touches. The Narutis Hotel also features a spa, sauna, and a well-regarded restaurant. It's located on Pilies Street, a short walk from the Cathedral Square Christmas tree, Vilnius University, and several other key attractions.

5. Stikliai Hotel

Address: Gaono g. 7, Vilnius 01131

Price Range: €170-€300 per night

Contact: +370 5 264 9595 | reservations@stikliaihotel.lt

Description: This charming, five-star boutique hotel is located in Vilnius' historic Jewish quarter.

The Stikliai Hotel combines luxury with intimacy, offering elegantly decorated rooms and suites, a spa, and gourmet dining at its restaurant.

A cozy spot to retreat to after a day of exploring the city's Christmas lights and festive atmosphere, the hotel's location places it within walking distance of the Christmas markets and main attractions like the Presidential Palace.

Mid-Range Accommodations: Comfort and Value

Vilnius offers plenty of mid-range accommodations that balance comfort with value, perfect for travelers who want excellent service and amenities without breaking the bank.

1. Hotel Congress Avenue

Address: Gedimino pr. 12, Vilnius 01103

Price Range: €90-€140 per night

Contact: +370 5 266 8200 | info@congressavenue.lt

Description: Located on Vilnius' main boulevard, this modern and stylish hotel offers spacious rooms with all the amenities you need for a comfortable stay. It's conveniently located near the Lithuanian National Opera and Ballet Theatre and just a 10-minute walk from Cathedral Square's Christmas festivities.

2. Artis Centrum Hotels

Address: Totorių g. 23, Vilnius 01120

Price Range: €80-€130 per night

Contact: +370 5 266 0366 | info@artis.centrumhotels.com

Description: With a charming blend of classic and modern design, Artis Centrum Hotel is housed in a historic building near the Presidential Palace. The hotel offers a wellness center with a sauna and swimming pool, and its restaurant serves traditional Lithuanian dishes. It's a short walk to the main Christmas market and the picturesque Old Town streets.

3. Novotel Vilnius Centre

Address: Gedimino pr. 16, Vilnius 01103

Price Range: €80-€120 per night

Contact: +370 5 266 6200 | H5209@accor.com

Description: Novotel Vilnius Centre is a well-known international hotel offering comfort and reliability in the heart of the city. The hotel features modern rooms with excellent views of the city, a fitness center, and a family-friendly atmosphere. Its location makes it easy to access the city's holiday attractions, with the main Christmas market just a 10-minute walk away.

4. Amberton Cathedral Square Hotel

Address: L. Stuokos-Gucevičiaus g. 1, Vilnius 01122

Price Range: €90-€140 per night

Contact: +370 5 210 7461 | info@ambertonhotels.com

Description: With unbeatable views of Cathedral Square and its iconic Christmas tree, Amberton offers an ideal location for holiday travelers. Rooms are modern and comfortable, and the hotel's restaurant serves both international and Lithuanian cuisine. The location is perfect for walking to Vilnius' top attractions, including Gediminas Tower and the Old Town.

Budget-Friendly Stays: Hostels, Guesthouses, and Affordable Hotels

For budget-conscious travelers, Vilnius has plenty of affordable options that don't compromise on quality or comfort. Here are some of the best value-for-money accommodations:

1. Downtown Forest Hostel & Camping

Address: Paupio g. 31A, Vilnius 11341

Price Range: €20-€40 per night

Contact: +370 5 265 2550 | stay@downtownforest.lt

Description: This quirky and cozy hostel is located in a quieter area near the Bernardine Gardens but still within walking distance of Vilnius' main attractions. It offers both dormitories and private rooms, and has a relaxed, friendly atmosphere. Perfect for budget travelers who still want to experience the Christmas charm of Vilnius.

2. Jimmy Jumps House Hostel

Address: Saviciaus g. 12-1, Vilnius 01127

Price Range: €12-€30 per night

Contact: +370 5 212 2940 | jimmyjump@gmail.com

Description: One of Vilnius' most popular hostels, Jimmy Jumps offers dormitory accommodation with a lively social atmosphere. It's a great base for younger travelers looking to experience Vilnius on a budget. The hostel is a short walk from the main Christmas markets and Vilnius' nightlife.

3. Ibis Vilnius Centre

Address: Rinktinės g. 18, Vilnius 09310

Price Range: €50-€80 per night

Contact: +370 5 262 0700 | H9572@accor.com

Description: A budget-friendly option that offers excellent value for money, Ibis Vilnius Centre provides comfortable rooms and modern amenities. Located close to the river and only a short walk to the city center, it's a great choice for those wanting to explore Vilnius' Christmas attractions without overspending.

Unique Stays: Boutique Hotels and Airbnb Options

Vilnius also has a range of boutique hotels and Airbnb properties that offer unique, personalized experiences for travelers looking for something different during their Christmas stay.

1. Shakespeare Boutique Hotel

Address: Bernardinų g. 8/8, Vilnius 01124

Price Range: €120-€180 per night

Contact: +370 5 266 5885 | info@shakespeare.lt

Description: This charming boutique hotel is housed in a 17th-century building and features individually themed rooms inspired by literary figures. With its cozy library, classic décor, and a warm ambiance, it's perfect for a romantic Christmas escape. Its location in the Old Town makes it easy to explore Vilnius' Christmas markets and historical sights.

2. Vilnius Boutique Apartments

Address: Various locations around the Old Town

Price Range: €60-€100 per night

Contact: +370 616 31706 | vilniusapartments@gmail.com

Description: These modern apartments offer a more home-like experience for travelers looking for independence during their stay. Situated in or near the Old Town, they are well-equipped for longer stays and provide easy access to Christmas attractions, shops, and restaurants.

Christmas-Themed Stays: Hotels and Stays with Special Festive Packages

For those who want to fully immerse themselves in the Christmas spirit, some hotels offer special festive packages that include holiday-themed decorations, Christmas Eve dinners, and more.

1. Grand Hotel Kempinski Vilnius

Address: Universiteto g. 14, Vilnius 01122

Price Range: €300-€450 per night during Christmas

Description: The Grand Hotel Kempinski offers exclusive Christmas packages, including festive dinners at the on-site restaurant, Christmas Eve events, and a lavishly decorated lobby. Guests can enjoy special seasonal spa treatments and panoramic views of the Cathedral Square Christmas tree.

2. Radisson Blu Hotel Lietuva

Address: Konstitucijos pr. 20, Vilnius 09308

Price Range: €100-€160 per night

Contact: +370 5 272 6272 | info.lietuva.vilnius@radissonblu.com

Description: Radisson Blu Hotel Lietuva offers a memorable Christmas experience with its special holiday package. Guests can enjoy a festive breakfast buffet featuring seasonal treats, while the hotel is adorned with beautiful Christmas decorations, creating a warm and inviting holiday atmosphere. The hotel also offers discounted rates for its spa treatments, providing a relaxing escape during the busy holiday season. Conveniently located near the Neris River, the hotel is within walking distance of Vilnius' major attractions, including the Christmas markets and the historical Old Town. This makes it an ideal stay for those wanting to be close to both festive celebrations and sightseeing opportunities.

3

Vilnius Christmas Markets

Vilnius transforms into a magical destination during Christmas, with its streets and squares illuminated by twinkling lights and adorned with festive decorations. The heart of the holiday season lies in its vibrant Christmas markets, where locals and tourists alike gather to experience the spirit of the season. One of the most iconic Christmas markets in Vilnius is the Cathedral Square Christmas Market, but other smaller markets and events also dot the city, each offering a unique take on Lithuanian holiday traditions.

Cathedral Square Christmas Market

Location: Cathedral Square, Vilnius Old Town

Dates: Usually runs from late November to early January

Hours: Typically open from 11:00 AM to 8:00 PM (weekdays) and until 10:00 PM on weekends

The Cathedral Square Christmas Market is the crown jewel of holiday festivities in Vilnius. Located in the historic Old Town, it's set against the stunning backdrop of Vilnius Cathedral and the towering Christmas tree, which is regarded as one of the most impressive in Europe. The tree itself is a work of art, changing its theme each year to captivate visitors. Surrounding it, wooden stalls are set up in a charming village-like layout, offering a delightful array of Christmas goods, from handcrafted items to traditional Lithuanian holiday treats.

Key Features: Crafts, Food, and Entertainment

Crafts and Artisanal Goods

One of the main draws of the Cathedral Square Christmas Market is the opportunity to purchase unique, handcrafted items from local artisans. The market stalls feature a wide range of products, many of which reflect Lithuania's rich cultural heritage. Traditional items include woolen goods like scarves, mittens, and sweaters, perfect for the cold winter season. You'll also find beautifully crafted wooden toys, hand-painted Christmas ornaments, and intricately designed amber jewelry, which is a signature Lithuanian craft. These unique, locally-made gifts make for thoughtful souvenirs or presents for loved ones.

Festive Food and Drinks

The Cathedral Square market is also a paradise for food lovers, with vendors offering a variety of traditional Lithuanian dishes and holiday treats. Some of the must-try foods include cepelinai (potato dumplings filled with meat or cheese), kūčiukai (tiny, crunchy pastries typically eaten during Christmas Eve dinner), and šakotis, a spiky tree-shaped cake that's as delicious as it is visually striking. For something warm, try kepta duona, fried bread with garlic and cheese, a beloved Lithuanian snack.

For those in the mood for something sweet, you'll find an array of gingerbread cookies, cakes, and chocolates. Pair these treats with a cup of karštas vynas (mulled wine) or gira, a traditional Lithuanian beverage made from fermented bread, to complete the festive experience.

Live Entertainment and Festivities

The Cathedral Square Christmas Market is more than just a place to shop—it's a hub of holiday entertainment. Throughout the season, the square hosts a variety of performances, from traditional Lithuanian folk music and dance to live concerts featuring choirs and orchestras. Visitors can also enjoy carol singing and watch theatrical performances of Christmas stories.

A highlight for families is the arrival of Kalėdų Senelis (Santa Claus), who greets children and spreads Christmas cheer. There are often special workshops where children can participate in activities like cookie decorating or making their own Christmas ornaments. The atmosphere is alive with the sounds of Christmas music, creating a heartwarming experience for all who visit.

Unique Christmas Gifts to Look Out For

Vilnius' Christmas markets offer the perfect opportunity to find one-of-a-kind gifts for friends and family. Some of the most popular and unique items include:

Amber Jewelry: Lithuania is famous for its Baltic amber, often referred to as "Lithuanian gold." At the market, you'll find an array of amber necklaces, bracelets, earrings, and other items. Each piece of amber is unique, and some even contain ancient insects or plant life fossilized inside, making it a truly special gift.

Handmade Woolen Goods: Lithuania has a long tradition of wool craftsmanship, and you'll find beautifully knit scarves, hats, gloves, and socks.

These warm and cozy items are not only practical for the winter season but are often intricately patterned with traditional Lithuanian designs.

Lithuanian Ceramics: Ceramic mugs, bowls, and plates are popular items at the market, often decorated with traditional folk motifs. These handcrafted pieces are perfect for those who enjoy collecting unique, artisanal homeware.

Wooden Crafts: Another popular craft in Lithuania is woodwork. At the market, you can purchase intricately carved wooden figurines, toys, and even small pieces of furniture. Many of the items reflect Lithuanian nature and wildlife, making them a charming keepsake from your trip.

Traditional Christmas Ornaments: For those looking to add a touch of Lithuania to their Christmas tree, the market offers a variety of handcrafted ornaments. These can range from delicate straw stars, inspired by traditional Lithuanian holiday decorations, to more modern glass baubles painted with scenes from Vilnius.

Scented Candles and Soaps: Handmade candles and natural soaps infused with local herbs and essential oils make for wonderful gifts. Many of these products are made from eco-friendly materials and are packaged beautifully, ready to be gifted.

Whether you're strolling through the Cathedral Square Christmas Market or exploring some of the smaller markets around the city, Vilnius offers a magical Christmas shopping experience. The combination of unique gifts, delicious food, and festive entertainment ensures that visitors will leave with cherished memories and special souvenirs that capture the spirit of a Lithuanian Christmas.

Bernardine Garden Market

The Bernardine Garden Market is a smaller, more intimate Christmas market nestled within one of Vilnius' most picturesque parks, just behind St. Anne's Church and the Vilnius University Botanical Garden. This market, while less crowded than the one at Cathedral Square, offers an authentic and relaxed holiday atmosphere. With the tranquil surroundings of the Bernardine Gardens, this market provides an ideal spot for visitors to immerse themselves in the spirit of a traditional Lithuanian Christmas, away from the hustle and bustle of the city center.

Traditional Lithuanian Crafts and Food

At the Bernardine Garden Market, you'll discover a rich selection of traditional Lithuanian crafts, made by local artisans who continue centuries-old traditions. Among the standout crafts are woven tapestries, straw ornaments, and intricate wooden carvings. These crafts reflect Lithuania's deep connection to nature and its folklore, making them unique keepsakes or gifts for loved ones back home. Many of these handmade goods are rooted in ancient Baltic traditions, offering a glimpse into Lithuania's cultural heritage.

The market also offers traditional Lithuanian food, including hearty dishes that have been enjoyed for generations. Visitors can try kibinai, savory pastries filled with meat or vegetables, or kugelis, a traditional potato pudding that's a favorite among locals. Don't miss the mead (honey wine), a drink with historical significance in Lithuania, as it was once served at royal feasts.

During Christmas, vendors often sell special holiday versions of šakotis (spit cake) and gingerbread cookies, which make for delicious edible souvenirs.

Family-Friendly Attractions

The Bernardine Garden Market is especially popular with families, thanks to its quieter setting and variety of kid-friendly attractions. Children can enjoy interactive craft workshops, where they can learn to make their own Christmas decorations, such as traditional straw ornaments or hand-painted wooden toys. These activities offer a hands-on way for children to engage with Lithuanian traditions, while giving parents a chance to shop or enjoy the festive surroundings.

In addition to crafts, the market often features live performances tailored for families, such as puppet shows and storytelling sessions about Christmas legends. The natural setting of Bernardine Garden also provides ample space for families to take a leisurely stroll along the park's paths, many of which are decorated with lights and holiday displays.

Smaller, Local Markets: Hidden Gems for Authentic Experiences

Beyond Bernardine Garden, Vilnius boasts a number of smaller, local Christmas markets, each offering a more intimate and authentic experience compared to the larger, more commercial markets. These hidden gems are often located in neighborhoods or near local landmarks, where residents shop for handcrafted goods, holiday decorations, and locally produced foods.

One such market is held at **Lukiškės Square**, a historic spot that transforms into a festive marketplace during the Christmas season. This market is known for its focus on handmade gifts and local produce, and you'll often find items here that aren't available in the larger markets. Local bakers sell their freshly made breads and cakes, while vendors offering organic honey, jams, and preserves are popular among those looking for artisanal, high-quality gifts.

Local Artisans and Products

The smaller markets are where you're most likely to find local artisans showcasing their handcrafted wares, from ceramic bowls and leather goods to hand-stitched linens and jewelry made from Baltic amber. Each artisan takes great pride in their craft, and visitors often have the chance to meet them in person, hearing the stories behind the products they create. This personal connection, along with the quality and authenticity of the items, makes shopping at these local markets a truly unique experience.

For those interested in more contemporary Lithuanian products, some of these smaller markets also feature modern Lithuanian designers, offering innovative takes on traditional crafts. Whether it's a minimalist wooden ornament or a sleek piece of amber jewelry, these designs blend the old with the new, providing a fresh perspective on Lithuanian craftsmanship.

At the heart of these markets is a sense of community and tradition, with many of the products being passed down through generations.

Supporting these artisans not only ensures that these traditions continue, but also offers travelers the chance to take home a piece of Lithuanian culture that has been made with care and craftsmanship.

Whether you're visiting the Bernardine Garden Market, exploring smaller neighborhood markets, or browsing stalls at Lukiškės Square, you'll be treated to a rich selection of authentic Lithuanian crafts, foods, and holiday experiences. These smaller markets offer a more relaxed, personal encounter with Lithuanian culture during the Christmas season, perfect for travelers who want to experience a less touristy, more local side of Vilnius.

Top Christmas Attractions in Vilnius

The city of Vilnius comes alive during the holiday season, offering a variety of Christmas attractions that blend tradition, history, and festive cheer. From its iconic Christmas tree to religious services at the grand cathedral, Vilnius provides something for every traveler looking to experience the magic of a Lithuanian Christmas.

a. The Vilnius Christmas Tree

History and Location

The Vilnius Christmas Tree has become a symbol of the city's festive season and is widely recognized as one of the most beautiful Christmas trees in Europe. Located in Cathedral Square, right in the heart of the city, the Christmas tree tradition dates back decades, but in recent years, the tree's design has gained international attention. Each year, the tree is transformed with a new, creative theme, which often reflects elements of Lithuanian culture, history, or modern artistic trends.

Annual Themes and Lighting Ceremony

The lighting ceremony of the Vilnius Christmas Tree is one of the most anticipated events of the season. Typically held in late November, the ceremony is accompanied by music, performances, and a gathering of locals and tourists. The themes are kept under wraps until the big reveal, making the event even more exciting. Past themes have included intricate designs made from natural materials, innovative light displays, and even environmentally conscious decorations using recycled materials.

Getting There

The tree is centrally located in Cathedral Square in the Old Town, making it easy to reach by public transportation, taxi, or even on foot if you're staying nearby. It's within walking distance from Gediminas Avenue and the Vilnius Old Town.

Address: Cathedral Square, Vilnius 01143

Public Transit: Bus routes 1G, 2G, 10, 11, 88

Contact: Vilnius Tourism Office (+370 5 212 2595)

Why Visit

Visitors flock to see the Christmas tree not just for its beauty but for the surrounding festivities, including market stalls, caroling, and holiday performances. The square becomes a hub for outdoor activities, from ice skating to shopping for handmade gifts.

Pro Tip: Visit after sunset to see the tree fully illuminated, and time your visit during one of the Christmas concerts often held in the square.

Don't Miss

The annual Christmas Village that springs up around the tree, offering local crafts, foods, and holiday gifts. Grab a warm mulled wine and enjoy the festive atmosphere while admiring the tree from various angles.

b. Cathedral Basilica of St. Stanislaus and St. Ladislaus

History and Significance

The Cathedral Basilica of St. Stanislaus and St. Ladislaus is not only the heart of religious life in Vilnius but also an architectural marvel with deep historical roots. It has been the site of numerous significant events in Lithuania's history, including royal coronations and state ceremonies. The cathedral dates back to the 13th century and has undergone several restorations, with its current neoclassical appearance being a result of 18th-century renovations.

Midnight Mass and Religious Services

During the Christmas season, the cathedral is a central location for religious celebrations. The Midnight Mass on Christmas Eve is one of the most significant events, drawing locals and visitors alike. The service is conducted in multiple languages and celebrates the traditions of both Lithuanian Catholics and other Christian denominations. In addition to midnight mass, the cathedral holds several services throughout the season, including special events for Epiphany and the New Year.

Getting There

The cathedral is located at the end of Gediminas Avenue, right next to Cathedral Square, making it an easy walk from the Christmas markets and main tourist areas.

Address: Katedros a. 1, Vilnius 01143

Public Transit: Buses 11, 33, 88

Contact: +370 5 261 1127

Admission: Free, donations are welcome.

Opening Hours

Monday – Sunday: 7:30 AM – 6:30 PM

Midnight Mass: Starts at 12:00 AM on Christmas Eve

Why Visit

Aside from its religious significance, the cathedral's towering columns and classical design make it a must-see attraction. Inside, visitors can marvel at the stunning frescoes, altars, and sculptures, while those interested in history can take a guided tour of the catacombs, which hold the tombs of Lithuanian royalty and aristocracy.

Outdoor Activities

The Cathedral Square, which surrounds the basilica, is often the site of open-air concerts and Christmas processions. The square is lively during the holiday season, with visitors gathering around the tree or exploring the nearby market.

Pro Tip: Arrive early for Midnight Mass, as the cathedral fills up quickly. If you can't make it inside, the service is often broadcast on a screen outside, so you can still participate in the celebrations.

Don't Miss

Climb the Bell Tower of the cathedral for panoramic views of the city and the Christmas tree in Cathedral Square. During December, the views are particularly magical, with Vilnius bathed in holiday lights.

c. Christmas Concerts and Events

In addition to religious services, the Cathedral Basilica is home to numerous Christmas concerts throughout the holiday season. Local choirs, orchestras, and international performers often use the basilica's excellent acoustics to put on festive performances. These concerts typically feature a mix of traditional Lithuanian Christmas carols, classical music, and contemporary pieces.

Admission Fees: Some concerts are free, while others may charge between €10 and €30 depending on the performance.

Tickets and Schedule: Tickets for paid concerts can be purchased at the cathedral or through the official website. For a schedule of events, check the Vilnius Tourism Office or the basilica's calendar.

Why Visit

The Christmas concerts at the basilica are not to be missed, as they offer a peaceful respite from the bustling markets and commercial areas. The cathedral's grand architecture and serene ambiance create the perfect setting for reflecting on the season's meaning through music.

Pro Tip: If you're visiting with children, look for special family-friendly performances, including choir events and nativity plays that are shorter and more interactive.

Don't Miss

The annual Christmas Oratorio, a classical music event performed by a local orchestra and choir, is a standout concert that celebrates the beauty and solemnity of the season.

Whether you're admiring the stunning Vilnius Christmas Tree, attending a midnight mass, or enjoying a concert at the Cathedral Basilica of St. Stanislaus and St. Ladislaus, the city's top Christmas attractions offer a mix of cultural, historical, and festive experiences that are sure to enchant every traveler during the holiday season.

d. Gediminas Tower

Winter Views Over Vilnius

Gediminas Tower, standing proudly atop **Castle Hill**, offers one of the best panoramic views of Vilnius, especially during the winter months. Covered in a light dusting of snow, the city's medieval rooftops and Baroque churches transform into a winter wonderland. The tower itself is a remnant of the once-formidable Upper Castle, with roots tracing back to the 15th century. Visiting during December allows you to enjoy crisp, clear skies that provide an unparalleled perspective over the snow-covered Old Town and the sprawling modern parts of Vilnius beyond.

From the top, you can spot the festive glow of Cathedral Square and the iconic Vilnius Christmas Tree below, as well as the winding streets lit up with holiday lights. Winter may bring a chill, but the peaceful, snowy views are worth the trek up the hill, rewarding visitors with an unparalleled snapshot of the city's past and present.

Evening Lights and Festive Atmosphere

While Gediminas Tower is stunning by day, it takes on a different character at night when the city is lit up for Christmas. The tower's hilltop location gives you a unique vantage point over Vilnius' glowing streets, twinkling Christmas trees, and the illuminated facades of its historic buildings. Castle Hill itself is often decorated with lights, adding to the magical atmosphere.

On winter evenings, the calm and serenity at Gediminas Tower make it the perfect spot to escape the busy streets below and enjoy a quiet moment of reflection. Wrap up warm, and take in the beauty of the city glowing in the soft light of the holiday season.

Getting There

You can access Gediminas Tower either by foot via a steep path that winds up Castle Hill or by taking the funicular for a small fee. The walk takes about 10-15 minutes, depending on the weather.

Address: Arsenalo g. 5, Vilnius 01143

Admission: Adults €5, Students €2.50

Opening Hours: Monday – Sunday: 10:00 AM – 5:00 PM

Contact: +370 5 261 7453

Pro Tip: Visit during the late afternoon to enjoy both the daytime and evening views. Be sure to dress warmly, as it can be windy at the top.

Don't Miss: The museum inside the tower, which details the history of Gediminas Castle and its importance in Lithuania's statehood. The exhibit also includes models and artifacts from the medieval period, adding a historical dimension to your visit.

e. Vilnius Old Town

Festive Decorations and Historical Charm

The Vilnius Old Town, one of the largest surviving medieval towns in Northern Europe, truly comes alive during the Christmas season. With its cobblestone streets and centuries-old buildings, the Old Town exudes a charming and nostalgic atmosphere. During the holidays, these streets are adorned with Christmas lights, garlands, and festive displays, creating a fairytale-like setting that enchants visitors and locals alike.

As you stroll through the Old Town, you'll notice how the decorations complement the city's historical architecture. Pilies Street, one of the main thoroughfares, is particularly picturesque, with lights strung across the narrow street, illuminating the facades of Gothic and Baroque buildings. The scent of mulled wine, gingerbread, and roasted chestnuts fills the air, inviting you to explore the various markets and shops that offer a wide range of traditional Lithuanian crafts and festive treats.

Must-Visit Spots for Christmas Lights

Several spots in the Old Town are must-visits for those seeking the best Christmas lights. The entire stretch of **Gediminas Avenue** is beautifully lit, providing a festive atmosphere as you make your way to Cathedral Square.

Don't miss **Town Hall Square**, which hosts its own smaller Christmas market and is often decorated with a dazzling light display, including a second, smaller Christmas tree that serves as a perfect backdrop for holiday photos.

Another unmissable spot is **Stikliu Street**, known for its bohemian charm. This narrow street, lined with artisan workshops and galleries, is lit up with twinkling lights, creating a cozy and magical atmosphere. It's a quieter, more intimate part of the Old Town, perfect for those looking to escape the crowds.

Getting There

The Old Town is easily walkable, and most attractions are within close proximity. Public transportation, such as buses and trolleybuses, can take you close to the edges of the Old Town, but the narrow streets are best explored on foot.

Address: Vilnius Old Town is bounded by Gediminas Avenue, the Neris River, and several key streets, including Pilies Street and Didžioji Street.

Public Transit: Bus lines 1G, 10, and 88 serve the Old Town area.

Pro Tip: While most visitors head to the Old Town during the evening to enjoy the lights, visiting early in the morning can offer a peaceful and more personal experience as the city awakens.

Don't Miss: Be sure to stop by St. Anne's Church, a Gothic masterpiece that is especially striking during the winter months.

The church's intricate facade is beautifully lit up at night, and its location near the Bernardine Garden Christmas Market makes it an ideal spot to visit after a stroll through the market.

With its historical charm and festive spirit, the Old Town and Gediminas Tower become magical destinations during Christmas. From breathtaking views to twinkling lights, these attractions offer visitors an unforgettable holiday experience steeped in both tradition and beauty.

 f. **The Palace of the Grand Dukes**

Christmas-Themed Tours and Exhibitions

The Palace of the Grand Dukes of Lithuania, a historical and cultural hub, offers an immersive experience for visitors interested in the nation's royal past, especially during the Christmas season. Originally built in the 15th century, the palace has witnessed significant moments in Lithuanian history, including the reign of the Grand Duchy of Lithuania. After extensive renovations, it reopened as a museum and cultural venue, providing a glimpse into the life of Lithuanian rulers, as well as the country's broader European connections.

During December, the palace hosts special Christmas-themed tours and exhibitions designed to showcase Lithuanian royal traditions around the festive season. Visitors can explore exhibitions that focus on how Christmas was celebrated at the royal court, with elaborate decorations, period costumes, and historical displays of Lithuanian holiday customs.

The tours are often accompanied by guides dressed in historical attire, bringing the stories of Lithuania's Grand Dukes and their Christmas traditions to life. There are also workshops where visitors can create their own traditional Lithuanian Christmas ornaments or bake festive treats.

Getting There

The palace is located in the heart of Vilnius, just a short walk from Cathedral Square. It's easily accessible on foot from most key areas in the Old Town, and public transportation is available nearby.

Address: Katedros a. 4, Vilnius 01143

Public Transit: Bus routes 1G, 2G, 11

Admission Fees: €8 for adults, €4 for students and seniors

Opening Hours: Tuesday – Sunday: 10:00 AM – 6:00 PM

Contact: +370 5 212 7476 | info@valdovurumai.lt

Why Visit

A visit to the Palace of the Grand Dukes during the holiday season provides a deeper understanding of Lithuania's royal heritage and the Christmas traditions that have shaped the nation's identity. The combination of historical insight and festive programming makes it an enriching experience for all ages. The palace itself, decorated with festive lights and seasonal exhibits, becomes even more magical in December.

Pro Tip: Plan to visit in the afternoon when the palace is quieter, and you'll have more time to explore the detailed exhibitions. Consider booking a guided Christmas tour for the full experience.

Don't Miss

The royal treasure exhibitions inside the palace, which feature jewels, weapons, and artifacts from Lithuania's rich royal past. These exhibits offer a unique glimpse into the opulence of Lithuania's ruling class, further enhanced during the Christmas season.

g. Vilnius TV Tower

Special Christmas Lighting and Views

Standing at a towering 326.5 meters, the Vilnius TV Tower is the tallest structure in Lithuania and an iconic part of the city's skyline. While the tower is impressive year-round, it becomes a must-see attraction during the holiday season due to its stunning Christmas-themed light displays. Each year, the TV Tower is transformed into what's often described as the world's tallest Christmas tree, with festive lights cascading down its sides to create a dazzling spectacle visible from miles away.

The holiday lighting ceremony usually takes place in early December, marking the start of the Christmas season in Vilnius. This impressive light display attracts locals and tourists alike, and viewing it from different parts of the city is an unforgettable experience.

The tower's lights change colors throughout the evening, synchronized to music and creating a festive atmosphere that adds to the Christmas spirit.

Getting There

Situated in the Karoliniškės district, the TV Tower is about a 20-minute drive from Vilnius Old Town. It's accessible by both public transportation and car.

Address: Sausio 13-osios g. 10, Vilnius 04347

Public Transit: Take buses 3G, 54, or 73 from the city center

Admission Fees: €8 for adults, €5 for children and seniors

Opening Hours: Monday – Sunday: 10:00 AM – 9:00 PM

Contact: +370 5 252 5333 | info@telecentras.lt

Why Visit

The Vilnius TV Tower is not only an architectural marvel but also offers breathtaking panoramic views of the city, especially during Christmas. Visitors can take the elevator up to the observation deck, located 165 meters above the ground, where you can enjoy 360-degree views of the snow-covered Vilnius landscape, glittering under the holiday lights. There's also a rotating restaurant, the **Paukščių Takas** (Milky Way), where you can enjoy a meal or warm drink while the tower slowly rotates, giving you a full view of the city.

Outdoor Activities

During the winter season, the TV Tower area often hosts outdoor skating rinks and other festive activities, making it a great destination for families and those looking to enjoy some holiday fun.

Pro Tip: Visit in the evening to fully appreciate the Christmas lights both on the tower itself and across the city. Arrive early to secure a table at the revolving restaurant, as it tends to get busy during the holiday season.

Don't Miss

The TV Tower Museum, located inside, offers an exhibition dedicated to the January 13, 1991 events, when Soviet forces attempted to take control of the tower during Lithuania's struggle for independence. It's a sobering but important part of Lithuania's history, providing context to the significance of the TV Tower beyond its holiday lights.

Vilnius Christmas Train: A Festive Ride Around the City

The Vilnius Christmas Train is one of the most beloved holiday traditions for both locals and visitors alike. This charming train, brightly decorated with Christmas lights and festive ornaments, offers a unique way to explore the city while immersing yourself in the holiday spirit. Starting at Cathedral Square, the train takes passengers on a leisurely tour through the beautifully lit streets of the Old Town and beyond, allowing riders to experience the festive atmosphere of Vilnius without the chill of walking.

As the train weaves its way through the city's narrow streets, passengers can enjoy views of the main Christmas attractions, including the Vilnius Christmas Tree, Town Hall Square, and other holiday light displays that adorn the Old Town. The ride is accompanied by festive music, which adds to the overall joyful mood of the experience. It's especially magical in the evening when the city's Christmas lights create a dazzling backdrop for the ride.

Getting There

The Christmas Train departs from Cathedral Square and runs regularly throughout the day, with more frequent rides in the evenings. Tickets can be purchased at the train's starting point or online.

Ticket Prices: Approximately €3 for adults and €2 for children

Schedule: The train typically runs from late November until early January, with rides every 30-45 minutes

Contact: +370 5 212 7777 (for schedules and ticket inquiries)

Pro Tip: Try to catch the train at sunset, when the lights begin to twinkle, but the sky is still light enough to see the historical buildings in full detail. Bundle up to stay warm during the ride!

Ice Skating Rinks: Where to Glide Outdoors

During the holiday season, several outdoor ice skating rinks pop up around Vilnius, giving visitors and locals the chance to enjoy some winter fun amidst the festive scenery. One of the most popular rinks is located in **Lukiškės Square**, where skaters can glide in the heart of the city, surrounded by seasonal lights and decorations. With music playing and the cold winter air biting at your cheeks, it's an idyllic way to experience Christmas in Vilnius.

Another popular skating location is at **Vingis Park**, where a larger rink offers a more expansive skating experience. The park, already a favorite spot for locals, becomes a winter wonderland in December, with trees draped in lights and a festive atmosphere that draws families and couples alike. Skates can be rented on-site, and there are often vendors nearby selling hot drinks and snacks to warm up after a skating session.

Key Ice Skating Locations

Lukiškės Square Ice Rink: Central location, ideal for visitors staying in the city center

Admission: €4, skate rentals available for an additional €2

Opening Hours: Monday – Sunday: 10:00 AM – 10:00 PM

Vingis Park Ice Rink: A more spacious and scenic option, great for families

Admission: €5, skate rentals available for €3

Opening Hours: Monday – Sunday: 10:00 AM – 9:00 PM

Pro Tip: If you visit during the evening, make sure to bring gloves and warm layers, as temperatures can drop significantly at night.

Don't Miss: For a special treat, visit one of the skating rinks during a weekend night, when they often host themed skate nights or live music events, adding even more magic to your Christmas holiday.

Christmas Concerts and Shows: Best Places to Experience Seasonal Music and Performances

Vilnius is home to a rich tradition of Christmas concerts and shows, which take place in various venues across the city during the holiday season. These events range from classical music performances in stunning historical settings to more modern shows and Christmas-themed productions. Whether you're a lover of traditional carols or contemporary Christmas music, there's something for everyone.

Cathedral Basilica of St. Stanislaus and **St. Ladislaus** is one of the most atmospheric venues for Christmas concerts. Known for its grand architecture and historical significance, the cathedral hosts several Christmas Eve and Christmas Day concerts, featuring choirs and orchestras performing beloved seasonal pieces. Midnight Mass, accompanied by a stunning choir, is a highlight for many, blending spirituality with the beauty of music in a sacred setting.

Another popular venue for seasonal performances is the **Lithuanian National Opera** and **Ballet Theatre**. During December, the theatre's calendar is packed with Christmas-themed ballets, such as The Nutcracker, and other festive performances. The theatre's beautiful interior and world-class performances make it a top destination for those seeking an elegant and cultural holiday experience.

For those looking for a more intimate setting, the **Vilnius Town Hall** often hosts smaller concerts, including performances by local choirs and chamber music groups. The Town Hall is beautifully decorated for the holidays, making it a cozy and charming spot to enjoy some Christmas music.

Key Venues for Christmas Concerts

1. **Cathedral Basilica of St. Stanislaus and St. Ladislaus**

Address: Katedros a. 1, Vilnius 01143

Admission: Free for religious services, concert ticket prices vary

Contact: +370 5 261 1127

2. **Lithuanian National Opera and Ballet Theatre**

Address: A. Vienuolio g. 1, Vilnius 01104

Admission: Tickets typically range from €10 to €50, depending on the show

Contact: +370 5 261 0707

3. Vilnius Town Hall

Address: Didžioji g. 31, Vilnius 01128

Admission: Prices for concerts range from €10 to €30

Contact: +370 5 261 8011

Pro Tip: Book your concert tickets in advance, as these events are popular and often sell out, especially for performances like The Nutcracker and the midnight concerts at the Cathedral.

Don't Miss: The annual Christmas Charity Concerts, which take place in various churches and venues across the city. These events are not only a chance to enjoy beautiful music but also an opportunity to give back, as the proceeds go to local charities and causes.

Winter Parades and Processions

Traditional Christmas Processions and Celebrations

During the Christmas season, Vilnius comes alive with vibrant winter parades and processions that showcase the city's rich cultural heritage and festive spirit. One of the most notable events is the Christmas Parade, which typically takes place in early December, marking the official start of the holiday season.

This lively event features colorful floats, traditional music, dance performances, and participants dressed in festive costumes that represent Lithuanian folklore and Christmas traditions.

The parade usually begins at **Cathedral Square**, winding its way through the streets of the Old Town. Families, tourists, and locals gather to enjoy the spectacle, with many people bringing their children to see Santa Claus and other holiday characters. The atmosphere is filled with joy and excitement, as the parade culminates in a celebration at the square, complete with live music, food stalls, and Christmas markets.

Another important procession is the **Epiphany Procession**, held in early January. This traditional event commemorates the visit of the Magi to the Christ child and involves a festive walk through the streets of Vilnius, where participants often carry candles and wear historical costumes. The procession is deeply rooted in religious significance, drawing together the community for a shared experience of faith and celebration.

Getting There

The Christmas Parade typically starts at Cathedral Square, making it easily accessible for those staying in the city center.

Schedule: Check local listings for specific dates and times, as they may vary each year.

Contact: For information on events, visit the Vilnius Tourism Information Center at +370 5 262 9660.

Pro Tip: Arrive early to secure a good viewing spot along the parade route, especially for the Christmas Parade. Bring along a thermos of hot chocolate to enjoy while you wait!

Don't Miss: The final festivities at Cathedral Square after the parade, where there's often live music, performances, and a chance to visit the Christmas market for unique gifts and seasonal treats.

Charity and Community Events

How to Participate or Support Local Charities During the Season

The holiday season is a time of giving, and Vilnius embraces this spirit through various charity and community events. Throughout December, numerous organizations and groups come together to support those in need, making it easy for visitors and locals alike to get involved.

One of the most popular initiatives is the **Christmas Charity Market**, typically held in Cathedral Square or another central location. Local artisans and vendors set up stalls to sell handmade crafts, festive foods, and holiday decorations, with all proceeds going to local charities and community projects. This market is a great opportunity to shop for unique gifts while supporting a good cause.

Additionally, many local churches and community centers organize food drives, where residents can donate non-perishable food items, clothing, and toys for families in need.

Participating in these drives is a meaningful way to contribute to the community during the holiday season.

Volunteering opportunities are also abundant, with many organizations seeking help for their holiday programs. Whether it's serving meals at a shelter, wrapping gifts for underprivileged children, or assisting with events, there are various ways to lend a hand.

Key Charity Events

Christmas Charity Market: Typically held in December; check local listings for exact dates and locations.

Food Drives: Ongoing throughout the holiday season at various churches and community centers.

Volunteering Opportunities: Contact local charities or community organizations to find out about specific needs and how to get involved.

Pro Tip: If you're visiting Vilnius during the holidays, consider bringing along a small donation—non-perishable food items or warm clothing are always appreciated.

Don't Miss: The sense of community and togetherness that these events foster. Engaging with local residents during these charity activities can provide a deeper understanding of Lithuanian culture and the spirit of giving that is so integral to the holiday season.

Participating in the winter parades and charity events in Vilnius not only enhances your holiday experience but also connects you with the local community and its traditions. Embrace the joy of giving and celebration that defines this magical time of year in the city.

Shopping for Christmas in Vilnius

Best Shopping Streets

Gediminas Avenue

One of the main arteries of Vilnius, Gediminas Avenue is the perfect place to start your Christmas shopping journey. Lined with a mix of high-end boutiques, international brands, and local shops, this vibrant street transforms into a festive wonderland during the holiday season. Visitors will find beautifully decorated storefronts, often featuring special holiday displays that make shopping here a joyful experience.

As you stroll along the avenue, don't miss the various pop-up shops that showcase local artisans and craftspeople, especially during the Christmas market season. Look out for traditional Lithuanian items like woolen sweaters, handmade jewelry, and leather goods. The atmosphere is lively, with cafes offering warm drinks and snacks to keep you energized as you shop.

Pilies Street

Adjacent to Gediminas Avenue, Pilies Street offers a charming cobblestone experience filled with unique boutiques and artisan shops. This historical street is famous for its quaint atmosphere and rich cultural heritage, making it a delightful place to shop for Christmas gifts. You'll find an array of handmade crafts, including ceramics, glassware, and artisanal food products.

Tourists should look out for small, family-run shops that often sell locally made goods, perfect for finding something truly special. Pilies Street is also home to several cafes and restaurants, providing ample opportunities to take a break and soak in the festive ambiance.

Shopping Centers and Boutiques

For those looking for a more extensive shopping experience, Vilnius has several shopping centers that offer a variety of options. **The Europa Shopping Center**, located a short distance from the city center, features a wide range of international brands, electronics, and a food court with both local and international cuisine. It's a great spot to find gifts for everyone on your list, from fashion to tech gadgets.

Another popular shopping venue is **Akropolis**, a large complex that combines shopping with entertainment. Alongside a multitude of shops, you'll find a cinema, bowling alley, and restaurants. During the Christmas season, Akropolis often hosts festive events, making it a lively destination for families.

Christmas Souvenirs and Gifts

When it comes to unique Lithuanian handicrafts, visitors will be delighted by the selection available throughout the city. Look for traditional items such as linen textiles, intricately designed wood carvings, and vibrant amber jewelry—Lithuania is renowned for its beautiful amber pieces.

Traditional Lithuanian Christmas Decorations are also a must-buy. Handmade ornaments, often crafted from natural materials like straw or wood, reflect the country's cultural heritage. Shops in both **Gediminas Avenue** and **Pilies Street** offer a variety of these decorations, including poppies, angels, and intricately painted wooden baubles.

Where to Buy Ornaments and Decor Items

Kalėdų Mugė (Christmas Market): Located in Cathedral Square, this market is a treasure trove for festive decorations and gifts. You'll find handcrafted ornaments, traditional sweets, and local delicacies, all while enjoying live music and entertainment.

Artisan Shops on Pilies Street: Several boutiques specialize in Christmas decorations, often featuring items made by local artists. Look for unique ornaments and handmade crafts that capture the essence of Lithuanian Christmas traditions.

What to Look Out For

As you explore Vilnius' shopping districts, be on the lookout for seasonal sales and special holiday promotions. Many shops offer discounts during the Christmas season, providing the perfect opportunity to snag gifts at a great price. Don't hesitate to ask shop owners about the stories behind their products; many are eager to share the cultural significance of their crafts.

Top Popular Shopping District

The Old Town of Vilnius is undeniably the top shopping district, where history meets modern shopping.

With its mix of traditional artisan shops, charming boutiques, and major retail outlets, it provides a diverse shopping experience against the backdrop of stunning architecture and festive decorations.

Shopping for Christmas in Vilnius offers an enchanting experience filled with unique gifts, traditional crafts, and a vibrant atmosphere. Whether you're wandering the streets, exploring shopping centers, or visiting Christmas markets, you're sure to find the perfect items to take home and share the spirit of the season.

Christmas Dining in Vilnius

Traditional Lithuanian Christmas Foods

Christmas in Lithuania is deeply rooted in tradition, and one of the most important elements of the holiday season is the food. The centerpiece of this celebration is Kūčios, the traditional Lithuanian Christmas Eve dinner, which holds great significance in both cultural and religious contexts. The meal is entirely meatless, consisting of 12 dishes, symbolizing the 12 apostles, and is prepared with a focus on simplicity and reflection. Kūčios is a time for families to gather and celebrate together, following age-old customs that have been passed down through generations.

Kūčios (Christmas Eve) Dinner: Traditions and Dishes

On the evening of December 24th, families across Lithuania sit down to the Kūčios meal. The table is often set with a layer of straw underneath the tablecloth, symbolizing the manger where Jesus was born, and an extra place is usually set for deceased family members or unexpected guests. Before the meal begins, it is common for the family to say a prayer or reflect on their blessings from the past year.

The dishes served at Kūčios are simple yet significant, with each one carrying its own meaning. Grain-based dishes, representing fertility and abundance, are central to the meal. Fish, particularly herring, takes the place of meat and symbolizes Christ's disciples.

The dishes are often prepared using natural ingredients such as grains, legumes, mushrooms, and root vegetables, emphasizing a connection to the earth and the cycle of life.

Popular Christmas Dishes to Try

Herring (Silkė)

Herring is a key dish during Kūčios, prepared in various ways, often with onions, carrots, or served in vinegar. It is symbolic of Christian fasting and humility, but the way it is prepared makes it flavorful and satisfying. Whether pickled, smoked, or served with vegetables, herring is a must-try dish during the Lithuanian Christmas season.

Kūčiukai

Perhaps the most iconic of all Kūčios dishes is Kūčiukai, small, crispy bread bites made from leavened dough, traditionally eaten with poppy seed milk. These bite-sized snacks are a symbol of the harvest and are typically prepared without sugar or other sweeteners, maintaining their simple and rustic nature. Despite their plainness, kūčiukai are deeply cherished as a representation of the essence of Lithuanian Christmas traditions.

Beet Soup (Barščiai)

Another staple of the Christmas Eve table is beet soup, known as barščiai, a warm, vibrant dish that brings color to the meal. Often served with dumplings or simply on its own, beet soup is light, nutritious, and perfectly suited to the meatless nature of Kūčios.

The slightly sour taste of the beets pairs well with the other, more neutral flavors on the table.

Poppy Seed Milk (Aguonų Pienas)

Traditionally consumed with kūčiukai, poppy seed milk is a unique and refreshing drink made from soaked and blended poppy seeds mixed with water. It is one of the most ancient and symbolic beverages of the Kūčios meal, often representing the hope for peace and fertility. The subtle flavor of poppy seeds offers a gentle, earthy contrast to the rest of the meal.

Dried Fruit and Nut Compotes

Lithuanians also enjoy dried fruit and nut compotes during Kūčios. These sweet, fragrant drinks are made by simmering a variety of dried fruits like apples, pears, and prunes with spices. The compotes are both warming and nourishing, providing a sweet end to the meal without violating the meatless nature of Kūčios.

Pyragas

To round off the meal, pyragas, a traditional sweet bread or cake, is often served. Although it is simple, pyragas is the perfect dessert for a Lithuanian Christmas, offering a subtly sweet, comforting taste that ties in with the meal's theme of modesty and reflection.

Pro Tip: While Kūčios dishes are traditionally homemade, several restaurants in Vilnius offer special Christmas Eve menus that include these dishes. If you're visiting Vilnius during the holiday season, make sure to try these traditional foods, as they provide a unique insight into Lithuania's rich cultural and religious heritage.

Don't Miss: Many bakeries and shops sell kūčiukai and other Christmas treats in the lead-up to the holiday. They make excellent snacks or gifts to bring home, offering a taste of authentic Lithuanian Christmas.

Christmas dining in Lithuania, particularly the Kūčios meal, is a celebration of tradition, reflection, and togetherness. The humble yet meaningful dishes that make up the meal provide a unique and memorable culinary experience for anyone visiting Vilnius during the festive season.

Top Restaurants for Christmas Dinner

During the Christmas season, dining in Vilnius becomes a special experience with many restaurants offering festive menus that blend traditional Lithuanian cuisine with international flavors. Whether you're looking to enjoy a classic Lithuanian Christmas meal or a more contemporary dining experience, there are numerous options that cater to every palate.

Recommendations for Both Traditional and International Cuisines

Lokys Restaurant

Address: Stiklių g. 8, Vilnius 01131

Contact: +370 5 262 9046

Price Range: €25-€40 per person

For those seeking an authentic taste of Lithuanian cuisine, Lokys is a must-visit. Known for its focus on game meats and hearty dishes, Lokys offers a special Christmas menu featuring traditional Lithuanian dishes such as roasted meats, potato dumplings, and wild mushroom sauces. The medieval-style decor and candlelit ambiance make it a cozy and festive place to celebrate Christmas with friends and family. During the holiday season, they often incorporate seasonal ingredients, providing a taste of Lithuania's ancient culinary traditions.

Pro Tip: Be sure to try their signature mushroom soup served in a bread bowl, a perfect winter dish that embodies the flavors of the forest.

Džiaugsmas

Address: Vilniaus g. 28, Vilnius 01402

Contact: +370 655 73444

Price Range: €40-€60 per person

For a more modern take on Lithuanian cuisine, Džiaugsmas is one of the top-rated restaurants in Vilnius, offering innovative dishes that use locally sourced ingredients. Their festive menu includes contemporary spins on traditional dishes, such as smoked duck breast with cranberry sauce or beetroot carpaccio. The sleek, minimalist decor contrasts with the warmth of the service and the beautifully presented dishes, making this a sophisticated option for a Christmas dinner.

Pro Tip: Džiaugsmas also offers a tasting menu that pairs perfectly with local wines. This is an excellent choice if you want to experience the full spectrum of flavors that Lithuanian ingredients offer.

Sugamour

Address: Vokiečių g. 11, Vilnius 01130

Contact: +370 620 77977

Price Range: €30-€50 per person

If you're in the mood for something sweeter, Sugamour is known for its delectable desserts and festive atmosphere. During the Christmas season, their menu features a variety of European-inspired holiday dishes and an extensive selection of pastries, cakes, and chocolates. It's a perfect spot for an indulgent Christmas dinner, followed by beautifully crafted desserts like gingerbread cakes or mulled wine macarons.

Pro Tip: Make sure to try their hot chocolate, which is rich and luxurious, perfect for a cold December night.

Festive Cafes and Bars: Cozy Spots to Warm Up with Mulled Wine, Coffee, and Christmas Treats

Coffee1

Address: Gedimino pr. 9, Vilnius 01103

Contact: +370 674 10766

Price Range: €5-€15

For a cozy, laid-back experience, Coffee1 is a favorite among both locals and tourists. This café offers a variety of seasonal drinks, including spiced lattes, mulled wine, and hot chocolate. They also feature Christmas-inspired treats such as gingerbread cookies and cinnamon rolls. The warm, inviting atmosphere with soft lighting makes it the perfect spot to take a break from the cold and enjoy a sweet snack. The location along Gediminas Avenue makes it convenient to stop by while shopping or sightseeing.

Pro Tip: Order the spiced latte with a side of their famous poppy seed cake, a local favorite during the holidays.

Vero Café

Address: Pilies g. 16, Vilnius 01123

Contact: +370 5 210 0004

Price Range: €10-€20

A popular local coffee chain, **Vero Café** is known for its specialty coffees and comfortable setting. During Christmas, they serve seasonal drinks like peppermint mochas and gingerbread lattes. It's a cozy spot to relax after a day of exploring the Christmas markets or enjoying the festive lights around the Old Town. Vero Café also offers an assortment of baked goods, including panettone and Christmas stollen, ideal for those with a sweet tooth.

Pro Tip: Try the peppermint mocha for a festive twist on your usual coffee routine, and pair it with a slice of seasonal fruitcake.

Šnekutis

Address: Polocko g. 7A, Vilnius 01205

Contact: +370 686 16433

Price Range: €10-€25

For a more casual and traditional experience, **Šnekutis** is a beloved Lithuanian pub known for its rustic charm and hearty fare. During the Christmas season, the pub often serves Lithuanian Christmas treats like kūčiukai and offers a wide selection of local beers and spirits. The homey, no-frills environment is perfect for warming up with a glass of hot mulled beer or spiced cider, both of which are popular seasonal choices. If you're craving more substantial food, the menu also includes traditional Lithuanian comfort dishes, such as cepelinai (potato dumplings) and roast pork.

Pro Tip: Try the mulled beer, a unique and warming drink that's perfect for experiencing the local flavor. Pair it with their deep-fried bread, a local snack that's often served as a bar treat.

Don't Miss: Many of the cafes and bars in Vilnius host live music or Christmas events during the holiday season, so keep an eye on local listings to enhance your festive dining experience. Additionally, most places offer holiday-themed desserts, such as Christmas cookies or Lithuanian honey cake, which are not to be missed.

Christmas dining in Vilnius offers a rich array of experiences, from traditional Lithuanian feasts to contemporary international cuisine. With plenty of cozy cafes and lively bars serving festive drinks and treats, the city is a food lover's paradise during the holiday season. Whether you're looking for a luxurious Christmas dinner or a simple spot to enjoy a warm drink, there's something for everyone to enjoy.

7

Winter Activities and Outdoor Adventures

The magic of winter in Vilnius extends beyond its festive markets and Christmas decorations. The city and its surrounding areas offer a wealth of outdoor activities and adventures, allowing visitors to embrace the winter season fully. Whether you prefer peaceful winter walks or thrilling snow sports, Vilnius has something for everyone.

Winter Walks in Vilnius Old Town: Scenic Routes and Must-See Spots

One of the most enchanting ways to experience winter in Vilnius is by taking a stroll through the UNESCO-listed Old Town, especially when the snow blankets the cobblestone streets and centuries-old buildings. The Old Town's charm intensifies during the Christmas season, with twinkling lights, festive decorations, and a serene atmosphere.

Key scenic routes include **Pilies Street**, one of the oldest and most vibrant streets in the city. Lined with historical buildings, cafes, and shops, it's a must-see during your winter walk. Take your time to admire **St. Anne's Church**, a Gothic masterpiece, and the nearby Bernardine Gardens, which offer a quiet winter retreat along the Vilnia River. The park is beautifully peaceful when dusted with snow, providing stunning views of the surrounding churches and the **Gediminas Tower**.

For panoramic views, make your way to **Subačiaus Street**, where the Vilnius Observation Deck provides a stunning winter vista of the Old Town's rooftops and church spires.

Pro Tip: Evening walks are especially magical as the streets are illuminated with soft Christmas lights. Don't forget to stop by Cathedral Square to see the iconic Christmas tree in all its splendor.

Sledding and Tobogganing: Best Hills for Snow Fun

Sledding is a popular and family-friendly winter activity in Vilnius. While there are no official sledding parks, the city's natural landscape provides plenty of opportunities to enjoy this thrilling pastime.

One of the best spots for sledding is **Vingis Park**, located along the Neris River. It's Vilnius' largest park, and its hilly terrain makes it perfect for both casual sledders and thrill-seekers. The park is a local favorite, and you'll find families and children enjoying the slopes throughout the day.

Another great spot is the **Belmontas** area (Pūčkorių atodanga), known for its scenic hills and proximity to nature. The area offers longer sledding paths with varying degrees of difficulty, making it a fun spot for both beginners and more adventurous sledders.

Pro Tip: If you don't have a sled, they are easy to rent at nearby shops or buy at supermarkets around Vilnius.

Cross-Country Skiing: Parks and Trails Around Vilnius

For cross-country skiing enthusiasts, Vilnius offers a variety of parks and green spaces that transform into snowy trails during the winter.

Vingis Park is one of the top spots for cross-country skiing, with its extensive trails winding through peaceful forests and open fields. The park is relatively flat, making it an excellent location for beginners to hone their skills. If you're more experienced, the park also has longer, more challenging trails that offer scenic routes along the river and through the woodlands.

Another popular destination for cross-country skiing is **Verkiai Regional Park**, located just north of the city. The park offers a mixture of forested trails and open spaces, allowing for a tranquil skiing experience. The snow-covered park, with its ancient oak trees and frozen ponds, provides a breathtaking backdrop for outdoor adventures.

Pro Tip: If you're new to cross-country skiing, equipment rentals are available at various sports shops around Vilnius, and guided tours are also available to help you get started.

Snowshoeing and Hiking: Explore Winter Landscapes Nearby

For those who prefer to explore on foot, snowshoeing is a fantastic way to experience Vilnius' winter landscapes. Snowshoeing is growing in popularity in Lithuania, and the parks surrounding the city offer plenty of opportunities to enjoy this activity.

Belmontas Park is an excellent option for snowshoeing, thanks to its rolling hills and forested trails. The park offers scenic views of the frozen waterfalls and snow-covered forests, making it an ideal winter destination for nature lovers.

Another great spot for snowshoeing is the Pūčkoriai Outcrop, a geological formation that provides excellent trails for a winter hike. The snow-covered landscape and panoramic views of the surrounding valleys and rivers make this one of the best places to enjoy a peaceful winter adventure.

Pro Tip: Dress in layers and bring a thermos of hot tea or coffee for your snowshoeing adventure. Local shops offer snowshoe rentals if you don't have your own equipment.

Day Trips from Vilnius

While Vilnius offers plenty of winter activities, taking a day trip to the surrounding regions adds an extra layer of adventure to your trip. Two top destinations to consider are **Trakai Castle** and **Neris Regional Park**.

Trakai Castle: Frozen Lakes and Christmas Spirit

Address: Kęstučio g. 4, Trakai 21104

Contact: +370 528 53941

Admission: €6-€8

Located just 30 kilometers from Vilnius, Trakai Castle is a must-see during winter. The medieval island castle sits majestically on Lake Galvė, which often freezes over during the colder months, creating a picturesque winter wonderland. The surrounding town of Trakai celebrates the Christmas season with decorations, markets, and events, making it a perfect day trip destination.

During winter, you can walk on the frozen lake (if the ice is thick enough) or take a stroll around the castle's exterior to admire its snow-covered towers. The castle often hosts Christmas-themed exhibitions and festive concerts, providing a historical and cultural twist to the winter experience.

Pro Tip: After exploring the castle, warm up with a cup of hot kibinai, a traditional pastry filled with meat or vegetables, available at local cafes nearby.

Neris Regional Park: Winter Wonderland

Address: Riešės sen., Vilnius 15140

Contact: +370 5 23 18 305

For nature enthusiasts, Neris Regional Park offers an escape into a tranquil winter landscape. Located just 25 kilometers northwest of Vilnius, the park's winter trails wind through snow-covered forests and along the frozen Neris River, creating an idyllic environment for hiking or cross-country skiing.

Winter in the park offers stunning views of the frozen river and the surrounding valleys. The park's vast forested areas are perfect for a quiet retreat, and the **Dūkštos Oak Forest** is one of the most scenic spots to explore during winter.

Pro Tip: Make sure to wear sturdy boots or rent snowshoes, as the trails can be icy. The park offers guided tours during the winter months, making it easier to navigate the snow-covered paths and learn more about the region's natural history.

Winter in Vilnius offers a diverse array of outdoor activities that cater to all interests, from peaceful walks through the Old Town to adventurous day trips to nearby castles and parks. Whether you prefer sledding, skiing, or simply enjoying the scenic beauty of a snow-covered landscape, Vilnius provides the perfect winter playground for travelers of all ages.

Religious and Cultural Traditions

Christmas in Lithuania, particularly in Vilnius, is deeply rooted in religious and cultural traditions that have been passed down through generations. The holiday season is not just about festive decorations and markets; it's a time when families come together to celebrate ancient customs that reflect the nation's strong Catholic heritage and folk traditions.

Christmas Eve (Kūčios) and Christmas Day Traditions: How Vilnius Families Celebrate

Christmas Eve, known as **Kūčios**, is the most important day in Lithuanian Christmas celebrations. This solemn and sacred evening is rich in symbolic customs, many of which reflect the country's agricultural past and strong religious faith. Kūčios is a time for family, with relatives gathering to share a traditional dinner that has deep spiritual significance.

The Kūčios meal traditionally consists of 12 dishes, representing either the 12 Apostles or the 12 months of the year. None of the dishes contain meat, as Christmas Eve is a day of fasting, in accordance with Catholic tradition. Typical dishes include herring, mushroom soup, boiled potatoes, poppy seed milk with kūčiukai (small, slightly sweet bread rolls), beetroot salad, and boiled peas.

Before the meal, it's customary to lay hay or straw under the tablecloth to symbolize the manger where Jesus was born. The meal begins after the first star appears in the sky, symbolizing the Star of Bethlehem, and the family exchanges consecrated wafers (**kalėdaitis**) as a gesture of peace and forgiveness.

Christmas Day is more festive, with a feast that includes various meat dishes like roasted pork or duck, alongside desserts such as **aguonų pienas** (poppy milk) and **šakotis** (a traditional Lithuanian tree cake). It's a day to celebrate the birth of Christ with loved ones, marked by joy, gift-giving, and festive meals.

Pro Tip: If you're staying with a local family or invited to a Kūčios meal, bring a small, thoughtful gift like traditional sweets or a candle as a gesture of goodwill.

Church Services and Midnight Mass: Key Churches for Religious Observances

Attending Midnight Mass (**Piemenėlių Mišios**) on Christmas Eve is a revered tradition for many Lithuanians. The Mass typically starts just before midnight, and churches throughout Vilnius are beautifully decorated with nativity scenes, candles, and Christmas trees, creating an atmosphere of reverence and joy.

The most prominent venue for Midnight Mass is the **Cathedral Basilica of St. Stanislaus** and **St. Ladislaus**, located in Cathedral Square. This church is the heart of the Catholic faith in Lithuania and holds a special place in the country's history. The Midnight Mass here is a spectacular event, drawing large crowds of both locals and tourists. The service, conducted in Lithuanian, is solemn yet uplifting, with traditional hymns and carols echoing through the grand cathedral.

Another significant church is **St. Peter and Paul's Church**, famous for its **Baroque architecture** and intricate interior. Attending Midnight Mass in this breathtaking church is a deeply spiritual experience, enhanced by the beauty of its ornate decor. **St. Anne's Church**, with its stunning Gothic exterior, also hosts Midnight Mass, offering a more intimate yet equally profound service.

Pro Tip: Arrive early to secure a seat, especially at the Cathedral Basilica, as Midnight Mass is extremely popular. Services typically last about an hour and are followed by warm greetings and festive celebrations among attendees.

Traditional Lithuanian Christmas Carols and Songs: Where to Hear or Participate

Christmas carols, known as **kalėdinės giesmės**, are an integral part of the Lithuanian Christmas experience. These songs, steeped in both religious and folk traditions, are sung in churches, at concerts, and even door-to-door in some rural areas, continuing an old tradition of koliada—caroling that dates back centuries.

Many carols reflect themes of joy, peace, and the birth of Christ, with some songs unique to Lithuania's Christmas folklore. Popular carols include **"Tyli naktis"** (the Lithuanian version of "Silent Night") and **"Džiaugsmingų Švenčių!"** (translated as "Joyful Holidays!").

During the Christmas season, several churches and concert halls host special performances of Christmas carols. The **Lithuanian National Philharmonic Hall** often holds a festive concert featuring traditional Christmas music, while the Vilnius Cathedral hosts choir performances where visitors can hear these ancient songs.

If you're interested in participating, some local community centers organize Christmas carol singing events, where locals and visitors alike are welcome to join in. These events are typically more informal and held in smaller neighborhood churches or cultural centers.

Pro Tip: Check local listings and event boards in December to find caroling events or concerts during your stay. Attending a traditional Christmas concert is a wonderful way to immerse yourself in Lithuanian culture and feel the true spirit of the season.

The religious and cultural traditions of Vilnius during Christmas create an atmosphere of reverence and warmth, blending faith, family, and community. Whether you attend a Kūčios dinner, Midnight Mass, or a Christmas carol concert, these experiences offer a deep connection to Lithuania's rich history and spiritual heritage, making your visit during the holiday season truly unforgettable.

Family-Friendly Christmas Experiences

Christmas in Vilnius is a magical time for families, offering a wide array of experiences that bring out the wonder of the season, especially for children. From festive shows and workshops to visiting Santa and enjoying interactive exhibits, Vilnius turns into a wonderland where families can make lasting holiday memories together.

Children's Christmas Events: Shows, Workshops, and Special Activities for Kids

The Christmas season in Vilnius is filled with events specially curated for children. Numerous theaters and cultural centers around the city host Christmas-themed performances, including puppet shows, children's plays, and festive concerts designed to enchant younger audiences. One popular venue for family-friendly shows is the **Vilnius Puppet Theatre Lėlė**, which often stages delightful performances based on Lithuanian folklore or classic holiday tales.

Throughout December, there are also Christmas workshops where kids can get hands-on with crafting decorations, making gingerbread cookies, or writing letters to Santa Claus. These activities are not only entertaining but also give children a chance to engage in creative tasks while learning about Lithuanian holiday traditions. Many of these workshops are hosted in Vilnius Old Town, either at cultural centers or festive pop-up spaces near the markets.

Pro Tip: Keep an eye on Vilnius event listings, as many of these activities are free or reasonably priced, and workshops tend to fill up quickly, especially on weekends.

Santa's House in Vilnius: Where to Meet Santa and Enjoy Christmas Magic

One of the highlights for families visiting Vilnius during the festive season is a trip to Santa's House. This magical experience is usually set up in the Bernardine Gardens or in Cathedral Square, offering children the opportunity to meet Santa Claus, share their Christmas wishes, and take home memorable photos.

Santa's House is beautifully decorated, giving it a whimsical and magical atmosphere that delights visitors of all ages. Children can engage in small talks with Santa, who typically speaks both Lithuanian and English, making it a universal experience for tourists as well. Parents will appreciate the friendly environment and opportunities for professional family portraits.

Santa's House is generally open throughout December, with no admission fee, though it's a good idea to check opening hours and queue times. Be prepared to wait during peak holiday times, but the experience is well worth it for those magical moments with Santa.

Pro Tip: Visit Santa's House during weekdays or early mornings to avoid long lines. If you're there for a photo session, professional photographers are often available, but you can bring your own camera as well.

Interactive Museums and Exhibits: Family-Friendly Spots with Christmas Themes

For families looking to mix education with holiday fun, several museums in Vilnius feature interactive exhibits with a Christmas twist during the season. One notable destination is the **Toy Museum**, where children can explore vintage toys and participate in hands-on activities. During the Christmas period, the museum often features special exhibits related to holiday traditions from around the world, making it both entertaining and educational.

The **Lithuanian Energy and Technology Museum** also transforms into a family-friendly space during the holidays, hosting Christmas-themed exhibits that involve light displays, winter technology, and fun activities for children. Another option is the **MO Museum**, where families can often find festive art installations and kid-friendly workshops that invite younger visitors to engage with art through a holiday lens.

: The Toy Museum is an ideal stop for families with **Pro Tip** younger children, as they can touch and play with many of the exhibits, providing a hands-on experience that most museums don't allow.

The Vilnius Christmas Carousel: Rides for Kids in Cathedral Square

A magical addition to Vilnius' festive spirit is the charming **Christmas Carousel**, located in Cathedral Square. This enchanting ride, with its beautiful lights and traditional design, draws children and families from all over, providing a fun and memorable experience. The carousel is meticulously decorated with festive colors, and the gentle music playing in the background adds to the warm, nostalgic atmosphere.

The carousel is suitable for younger children, though parents can hop on alongside their kids to share in the experience. It's an ideal activity for families spending time in the heart of the city, especially as it's located near the iconic Vilnius Christmas Tree and the Cathedral Square Christmas Market, making it easy to combine this with other festive attractions.

The cost of a carousel ride is generally very affordable, with tickets available at a nearby kiosk. The carousel runs throughout December and into early January, operating well into the evening to allow families to enjoy the brightly lit square after dark.

Pro Tip: For a seamless visit, buy tickets in advance and enjoy a ride after visiting the nearby Christmas market. It's a great way to wind down after a day of exploring the festive streets of Vilnius.

Vilnius offers a wealth of family-friendly experiences that are sure to keep children entertained and parents engaged throughout the Christmas season. From magical encounters with Santa and festive rides to interactive museums and workshops, families can experience the joy and traditions of a Lithuanian Christmas while creating cherished holiday memories.

Vilnius at Night: Christmas Lights and Illuminations

During the holiday season, the streets, squares, and landmarks of Vilnius are transformed into a glittering wonderland of Christmas lights and illuminations. The city's nighttime scenery becomes a visual spectacle, making it one of the most magical places to explore after the sun sets. The captivating light displays and artistic installations throughout the city draw both locals and tourists alike, offering countless opportunities to take in the beauty of the holiday season.

Christmas Light Displays: The Most Spectacular Light Shows Around the City

One of the most awe-inspiring sights in Vilnius during Christmas is the Christmas tree in Cathedral Square, which is not just a tree, but a dazzling, themed light installation that stands as a symbol of the city's festive spirit. Every year, the tree follows a different artistic theme, incorporating thousands of lights, ornaments, and decorations that create an enchanting effect. Visitors can walk around the tree and admire its beauty from every angle, with the surrounding square also illuminated in warm, golden hues that evoke the essence of Christmas.

Vokiečių Street and **Gediminas Avenue** are two of the main thoroughfares that come alive with Christmas light displays. These streets are lined with festive lights that hang above, creating a canopy of sparkling decorations that make even a simple evening stroll feel like a festive occasion.

The Bernardine Gardens also hosts a beautiful display of lights, including glowing sculptures and lanterns that light up the pathways.

Another must-see during the season is the **Three Crosses Monument**, illuminated at night and offering panoramic views of the city's twinkling lights below. The monument is an iconic landmark that takes on a new level of beauty when surrounded by the glow of the city during Christmas.

Pro Tip: Check local listings for specific light shows or installations that might be unique to that year, as Vilnius often collaborates with artists to create special light displays and sculptures for the holiday season.

Evening Tours and Walks: Best Nighttime Routes for Viewing Christmas Lights

For those who want to fully experience the beauty of Vilnius at night during Christmas, taking an evening walk or guided tour is a must. The historic streets of Vilnius Old Town are some of the best routes for viewing the city's lights. Start your journey in Cathedral Square, where you'll be greeted by the Christmas tree and the illuminated Cathedral Basilica. From there, walk towards Pilies Street, where the old town's cobbled paths are beautifully lit with string lights hanging above, highlighting the charm of this UNESCO World Heritage site.

Continue your walk down to Town Hall Square, which often features its own smaller Christmas tree and light displays. The square is lined with festive stalls selling mulled wine and Christmas treats, and it serves as a hub for local celebrations and small concerts. Make sure to pass by the Presidential Palace, which is also elegantly illuminated at night during the festive season.

For a different perspective, take a stroll up to Gediminas Hill in the evening. As you make your way to the top, you'll be rewarded with stunning views of the city below, including the twinkling lights of Cathedral Square and the old town. If you're up for a more organized experience, there are several companies offering nighttime Christmas light tours, where a guide will take you around the best spots for holiday lights while sharing stories and insights about Vilnius's holiday traditions and history.

Pro Tip: Wear comfortable shoes and warm clothing for your evening walk, as temperatures can drop significantly at night. For a less crowded experience, try visiting the light displays on weekday evenings.

Photography Tips: Capturing the Best Christmas Scenes in Vilnius

Capturing the beauty of Vilnius at night during Christmas is a photographer's dream. With the city bathed in festive lights, there are endless opportunities to take stunning holiday photos, whether you're a professional or just using your smartphone.

However, photographing Christmas lights requires some attention to technique to truly capture the magic.

First, using a tripod is essential for stabilizing your camera or phone during long exposure shots, especially in low light conditions. Long exposure photography is perfect for capturing the twinkling lights and illuminated buildings, allowing you to collect more light in your photos and create sharp, vibrant images. Adjusting your ISO settings to a lower number will help reduce noise in your photos, while increasing the exposure time allows you to capture more light and detail.

When photographing the Christmas tree in Cathedral Square, position yourself at different angles to experiment with framing, using nearby landmarks like the Cathedral Basilica or Bell Tower as backdrops for your shots. Shooting from lower angles can also make the tree appear grander in your photos, while the golden glow of the surrounding lights will add warmth to your images.

Nighttime portraits are another great way to capture the Christmas spirit. Find a well-lit spot like Gediminas Avenue or Vokiečių Street, where the overhead Christmas lights create a festive atmosphere for portraits. Remember to use the lights as a backdrop, keeping the subject of your portrait illuminated by nearby sources of light like shop windows or lampposts.

Pro Tip: Explore more secluded spots like the Bernardine Gardens or the streets of Uzupis for unique, less crowded scenes.

These areas are often illuminated in a more subtle and artistic way, perfect for capturing more intimate or atmospheric holiday photos.

Experiencing Vilnius at night during Christmas is truly magical, with the combination of historical architecture, festive lights, and winter charm creating a captivating setting for visitors. Whether you're exploring the city's light displays, taking an evening stroll through the old town, or capturing the magic on camera, the city transforms into a winter wonderland that promises unforgettable holiday memories.

10

New Year's Eve in Vilnius

New Year's Eve in Vilnius is an unforgettable celebration, blending festive traditions with modern events, making it a fantastic place to ring in the new year. The city comes alive with fireworks, music, parties, and culinary delights, all against the backdrop of its historical charm and beautifully lit streets. From large public celebrations to intimate dinners, there's something for everyone.

New Year's Celebrations: Fireworks Displays and Events

The highlight of New Year's Eve in Vilnius is undoubtedly the midnight fireworks display, which typically takes place in Cathedral Square. As the clock strikes midnight, the sky over **Gediminas Hill** and **Vilnius Old Town** is illuminated with a dazzling array of fireworks that light up the entire city, offering a truly breathtaking sight. Thousands of people gather in and around Cathedral Square to watch the show, which lasts for several minutes, creating an electric atmosphere of excitement and celebration.

If you want a more panoramic view of the fireworks, consider heading to Three Crosses Hill or Gediminas Tower. Both locations offer spectacular vantage points, allowing you to take in the entire city and its fireworks displays from above. The atmosphere is festive but slightly quieter than the crowded streets below, making it a great choice for those who want to celebrate in a more serene setting while still enjoying the fireworks.

Throughout the evening, various events and street parties also take place around Vilnius. Many of these events feature live music, performances, and DJs, providing entertainment that leads up to the midnight celebrations. Lukiškės Prison 2.0, a creative venue set in a historic prison, often hosts unique New Year's Eve parties that blend culture, art, and music, drawing a more eclectic crowd.

Pro Tip: Arrive at Cathedral Square early to secure a good spot for the fireworks. If you prefer a more intimate viewing experience, pack a blanket, grab some hot drinks, and head to one of the city's higher vantage points for a less crowded view.

Top Venues for New Year's Parties: Where to Ring in the New Year in Style

Vilnius boasts an impressive variety of venues where you can ring in the new year in style, whether you're looking for high-energy parties, sophisticated soirees, or something in between. Vaidilos Theatre is one of the city's most elegant venues for New Year's Eve, often hosting a glamorous party with live music, cocktails, and dancing. The beautifully restored theater is an iconic spot, offering a sophisticated way to celebrate the new year.

For those seeking a more contemporary party atmosphere, **Loftas** is a popular choice. This industrial-style space, located in the Naujamiestis district, regularly hosts massive New Year's parties with top DJs, live performances, and creative art installations. The venue draws a younger, more energetic crowd, making it ideal for party-goers who want to dance the night away.

If you're after a luxurious experience, **Skybar** at the Radisson Blu Hotel Lietuva offers incredible views of the city's skyline, with a New Year's Eve party that features fine dining, craft cocktails, and a stylish atmosphere. The sweeping views from the 22nd floor make this one of the most sought-after spots to welcome the new year in Vilnius. Guests can enjoy an elegant dinner, then watch the fireworks from the comfort of the bar's plush interior.

Pro Tip: Make reservations well in advance, especially at popular venues like Skybar and Vaidilos Theatre, as they tend to fill up quickly for New Year's Eve.

Festive Dining and Midnight Toasts: Restaurant Recommendations for New Year's Eve Dinners

For a memorable New Year's Eve dinner in Vilnius, several top restaurants offer special menus that combine traditional Lithuanian flavors with modern cuisine, providing a festive yet refined dining experience. **Telegrafas**, located in the Kempinski Hotel Cathedral Square, is one of the most luxurious options for a New Year's Eve meal. The restaurant offers an elegant setting with views of Cathedral Square, and their New Year's Eve menu often includes delicacies like truffles, lobster, and high-end champagne for the midnight toast.

If you prefer a restaurant that blends tradition with innovation, **Džiaugsmas** is an excellent choice.

This award-winning restaurant is known for its creative takes on Lithuanian cuisine, using seasonal and local ingredients to create a modern, flavorful menu. For New Year's Eve, they usually offer a special tasting menu that showcases the best of Lithuanian gastronomy.

For a more casual yet festive atmosphere, **Ertlio Namas** in the heart of Vilnius Old Town offers a New Year's Eve menu steeped in Lithuanian history. The restaurant specializes in historical recipes reinterpreted for the modern palate, making it a unique dining experience that transports you through centuries of local food culture.

Pro Tip: Be sure to check the seating times for New Year's Eve dinners, as many restaurants offer an early dinner followed by a second seating that leads up to the midnight toast. Don't forget to make your reservations early, as spots fill up fast.

If you're looking for something more informal, the various Christmas markets scattered throughout the city remain open, serving up mulled wine, sausages, roasted nuts, and pastries. It's a perfect way to enjoy a relaxed evening outdoors before heading to a venue to ring in the new year.

Celebrating New Year's Eve in Vilnius offers an array of options, from vibrant street parties and fireworks to elegant dinners and luxurious venues. Whether you're looking to dance the night away or enjoy a gourmet meal before watching the fireworks, Vilnius provides the perfect setting for starting the new year in style.

11

Practical Information

When planning your Christmas trip to Vilnius, it's important to have all the practical details in place to ensure a smooth and enjoyable experience. Here's an extensive guide covering key aspects like visas, currency, emergency services, and language tips to help you navigate the city with ease.

Visas and Entry Requirements: Important Information for International Visitors

For international travelers, the entry requirements for Lithuania depend on your nationality. Lithuania is part of the Schengen Area, which allows passport-free travel between most European countries. This means that travelers from Schengen member states do not need a visa for short stays (up to 90 days).

For citizens of countries outside the **Schengen Zone**, such as the United States, Canada, Australia, and the United Kingdom, Lithuania allows visa-free entry for up to 90 days within a 180-day period, provided you are visiting for tourism or business. However, it's essential to have a passport valid for at least three months beyond your intended departure date.

For travelers from countries that are not part of the visa-exempt list, you will need to apply for a Schengen Visa. The process requires documentation such as proof of accommodation, travel insurance, financial means, and a travel itinerary. It's advisable to check with the Lithuanian embassy in your country well in advance of your trip to ensure all paperwork is in order.

Pro Tip: Lithuania uses the European Travel Information and Authorization System (ETIAS) for citizens from visa-free countries, so check if this applies to your nationality starting in 2025.

Currency, Payments, and Tipping: Guide to Money and Payments in Vilnius

The currency used in Lithuania is the Euro (€). When traveling to Vilnius, it's a good idea to have some euros on hand for small purchases like snacks, public transportation tickets, or at Christmas markets. However, most businesses, including restaurants, shops, and hotels, widely accept credit and debit cards.

ATMs are readily available across the city, and they accept most major international cards such as Visa, MasterCard, and American Express. Currency exchange offices can also be found at the airport, in large shopping centers, and around the old town. When withdrawing cash, it's advisable to check if your bank has any foreign transaction fees to avoid unnecessary charges.

In terms of tipping, Lithuania doesn't have a strong tipping culture, but it's appreciated in the service industry. For excellent service in restaurants, you can leave a 5-10% tip. Tipping taxi drivers and hotel staff is not obligatory but rounding up the fare or leaving a small gratuity is a nice gesture if you're happy with the service.

Pro Tip: Many Christmas markets, especially in smaller stalls, may only accept cash, so keep small denominations handy.

Emergency Services and Contacts: Health and Safety Information for Travelers

In case of emergencies, Lithuania has a well-developed emergency response system. The general emergency number is 112, which can be used for police, fire, and medical services across the country.

For medical assistance, Vilnius has several hospitals and clinics with English-speaking staff, especially in the larger institutions. **Vilnius University Hospital Santaros Klinikos** is one of the main healthcare facilities in the city and is equipped to handle emergencies. Pharmacies are widely available, often marked with a green cross, and many are open late or even 24/7.

It's recommended to have travel insurance that covers health emergencies, as medical treatment without insurance can be expensive. EU residents can use their European Health Insurance Card (EHIC) for medical services, but this only covers essential care, so additional travel insurance is still advised.

If you lose your passport or need consular assistance, the embassies for countries like the United States, United Kingdom, and other major nations are located in Vilnius. Keep a copy of your passport and important documents in case of loss.

Pro Tip: Keep local emergency contacts, such as your country's embassy in Vilnius, saved on your phone for easy access.

Language Tips for Visitors: Common Phrases and Useful Words in Lithuanian

Lithuanian is the official language of the country, and while English is widely spoken, especially in the tourism industry, learning a few Lithuanian phrases will enhance your experience and allow you to connect more easily with locals. Many young people and those working in hotels, restaurants, and shops speak English, but older generations may only speak Lithuanian or Russian.

Here are some useful phrases that will help you navigate Vilnius:

Hello: Labas (LAH-bahs)

Goodbye: Viso gero (VEE-so GEH-roh)

Please: Prašau (PRAH-show)

Thank you: Ačiū (AH-choo)

Yes: Taip (TYPE)

No: Ne (NEH)

Do you speak English?: Ar kalbate angliškai? (Ar KAL-bah-te AHN-glee-shkai)

How much does this cost?: Kiek tai kainuoja? (Kyek tay kai-NOO-oh-yah)

Where is the toilet?: Kur yra tualetas? (KOOR ee-RAH too-ah-LEH-tas)

If you're shopping or visiting a Christmas market, a few polite phrases like "Prašau" (please) and "Ačiū" (thank you) will be appreciated by the vendors. Similarly, when greeting locals or asking for directions, saying "Labas" (hello) creates a friendly and welcoming atmosphere.

Pro Tip: Download a translation app that works offline, like Google Translate, to help with any language barriers you may encounter while exploring the city.

This practical guide ensures that your trip to Vilnius during Christmas is stress-free. From understanding the visa requirements and currency to learning basic Lithuanian phrases and knowing emergency contacts, you'll be well-prepared to enjoy your holiday to the fullest.

12

Conclusion: Why Vilnius Is the Perfect Christmas Destination

As a Christmas destination, few places in Europe offer the magical blend of history, tradition, and modern festive flair that Lithuania's capital city provides. From the sparkling Christmas markets, rich cultural traditions, and festive decorations to the stunning winter landscapes and immersive religious experiences, Vilnius transforms into a winter wonderland that leaves a lasting impression on every traveler.

Recap of Highlights: Unique Christmas Experiences in Vilnius

One of the standout features of Vilnius at Christmas is the breathtaking Vilnius Christmas Tree, often heralded as one of the most beautiful in Europe. Placed in Cathedral Square, this tree is more than a holiday decoration—it's a work of art, carefully designed with annual themes that offer visitors something new each year. The lighting ceremony marks the official start of the festive season, drawing locals and tourists alike to witness the magical moment when the city truly comes to life.

Beyond the stunning tree, the Christmas markets are a must-visit. The main market in Cathedral Square offers a variety of unique gifts, from local handicrafts to delicious holiday treats. For those seeking a more intimate and authentic experience, the Bernardine Garden Market provides a cozy setting filled with traditional Lithuanian crafts and delicacies, perfect for sampling or bringing home as souvenirs.

The city's cultural and religious traditions also make Christmas in Vilnius a deeply meaningful experience. From the midnight mass at the Cathedral Basilica of St. Stanislaus and St. Ladislaus to the heartwarming community events, these moments capture the essence of Christmas in Lithuania. The country's devotion to Kūčios, the traditional Christmas Eve dinner, offers visitors a chance to taste the local flavors and experience a cherished family tradition.

For those seeking outdoor adventure, the nearby Trakai Castle, with its frozen lakes, provides an enchanting day trip, while activities like sledding, ice skating, and winter walks through the city's historic streets make it easy to embrace the season's beauty.

Final Tips for First-Timers: Making the Most of Your Christmas Vacation in Vilnius

To truly enjoy Christmas in Vilnius, first-time visitors should take the time to plan their visit around key events and attractions. Arriving early in the season, before Christmas Eve, allows travelers to experience the tree lighting, markets, and concerts while leaving time to explore the city's landmarks like Gediminas Tower and the historic Old Town.

When it comes to transportation, public transit is efficient, and the Christmas train offers a charming way to see the city. For accommodations, booking in advance is essential, especially for Christmas-themed hotels that offer festive packages.

Staying in the heart of the Old Town or near Gediminas Avenue puts you within walking distance of major attractions and the best Christmas lights.

Embrace the local customs—whether it's attending a midnight mass or trying traditional foods at the markets—and you'll walk away with a deeper understanding of Lithuania's festive spirit. Layer up for the chilly weather, and don't forget to explore the city's cozy cafes and mulled wine spots to warm up between outings.

From its twinkling lights to the welcoming hospitality, Vilnius during Christmas is an experience that combines the best of old-world charm and modern celebrations. Whether you're drawn to its cultural traditions, historic sights, or simply the magic of the season, a holiday here promises memories that will last long after the Christmas lights have been packed away.

13

Vilnius Sample Itinerary: A Magical Christmas Experience

Whether you have a long weekend or a week to explore, Vilnius is a destination that offers an array of experiences for every type of traveler. This sample itinerary focuses on the highlights of Vilnius during the Christmas season, ensuring you make the most of your festive vacation.

Day 1: Arrival and First Impressions

Morning: Arrive at Vilnius International Airport (VNO), which is conveniently located about 6 km from the city center. Transfer to your hotel via taxi or the city's efficient public transport. After checking into your accommodation—whether it's a luxurious 5-star hotel or a boutique stay in the heart of the Old Town—take some time to rest after your flight.

Afternoon: Start your exploration with a leisurely stroll around Vilnius Old Town, a UNESCO World Heritage Site. Head to Pilies Street to enjoy the festive atmosphere as it is adorned with holiday lights and Christmas decorations. The medieval charm of the Old Town will immerse you in the holiday spirit as you visit the many quaint boutiques and cafes along the way.

Evening: For dinner, savor traditional Lithuanian dishes at Lokys or Etno Dvaras, where you can try local specialties like cepelinai (potato dumplings) or kugelis (potato pudding). End your first day by visiting Cathedral Square, where the magnificent Vilnius Christmas Tree stands. If you're lucky, you might catch the evening light show or seasonal music performances.

Day 2: Christmas Markets and Cultural Landmarks

Morning: Start your day with a visit to Cathedral Square and explore the Vilnius Christmas Market, which offers everything from traditional Lithuanian crafts to festive foods like kūčiukai and spiced honey cakes. Browse for unique gifts or souvenirs, including hand-carved wooden items, ceramics, and cozy woolen products.

Midday: Visit the Cathedral Basilica of St. Stanislaus and St. Ladislaus, the spiritual heart of the city. This landmark is particularly special during the holiday season with its Christmas-themed decorations. If you're visiting around Christmas Eve, consider attending the Midnight Mass, a deeply moving tradition in Vilnius.

Afternoon: After lunch at Sugamour café (known for its elegant pastries and holiday cakes), take a short walk to Gediminas Tower, which offers panoramic views over the city. In winter, the snow-covered rooftops of Vilnius create a fairytale landscape. Afterward, explore Vilnius University, one of the oldest universities in Eastern Europe, and admire its historic courtyards.

Evening: For dinner, head to Dziaugsmas, a restaurant specializing in modern Lithuanian cuisine. Afterward, experience Vilnius at Night, exploring the city's illuminated streets and squares. Consider joining a guided Christmas lights tour, which takes you through the best-decorated streets and parks.

Day 3: Day Trip to Trakai

Morning: Take a day trip to Trakai, a charming medieval town located about 30 minutes from Vilnius by bus or train. Trakai is famous for its stunning Island Castle, which is especially magical in winter when the surrounding lakes freeze over. The castle hosts various Christmas-themed events and exhibitions, making it the perfect seasonal outing.

Afternoon: After exploring the castle, try the local specialty, Kibinai, a savory pastry filled with meat or vegetables, at one of Trakai's cozy lakeside restaurants. Spend the afternoon walking around the frozen lakes or, if you're adventurous, trying ice skating on the lake's surface.

Evening: Return to Vilnius in the late afternoon. For dinner, warm up at Mykolo 4, a cozy restaurant in Old Town offering delicious local dishes in a homely, festive atmosphere. Consider catching a Christmas concert or performance at one of the city's many venues, such as St. Catherine's Church or the Lithuanian National Philharmonic.

Day 4: Museums and Markets

Morning: Start your day with a visit to the Palace of the Grand Dukes of Lithuania, where you can explore Lithuania's royal history through immersive exhibitions and interactive displays. During Christmas, the palace often hosts themed tours and events that dive into Lithuanian Christmas traditions.

Afternoon: For lunch, stop by the Vilnius Food Hall, a trendy spot with a variety of options ranging from traditional Lithuanian dishes to international cuisine. Spend your afternoon shopping along Gediminas Avenue or Pilies Street, where you'll find a mix of designer shops, boutiques, and smaller Christmas markets offering handmade gifts.

Evening: Spend the evening exploring Bernardine Garden and its small Christmas market, which focuses on local artisans and food vendors. This market has a more intimate atmosphere, perfect for a quiet evening of shopping and snacking on Lithuanian gingerbread. For a memorable dining experience, reserve a table at Amandus, known for its Christmas tasting menu featuring seasonal ingredients and creative dishes.

Day 5: Outdoor Winter Fun

Morning: Begin your day with an invigorating walk through Neris Regional Park, just outside of Vilnius. The park transforms into a winter wonderland, ideal for snowshoeing or cross-country skiing. If you're not into skiing, a simple walk along its scenic trails offers stunning views of the snowy forests and frozen rivers.

Afternoon: For lunch, head back to the city and warm up with a bowl of Lithuanian beetroot soup at Senoji Trobele, a restaurant known for its rustic charm and hearty dishes. After lunch, head to one of the city's ice skating rinks, such as the popular outdoor rink in Lukiškės Square, where you can skate in the shadow of the Christmas lights.

Evening: End your day with a special Christmas-themed dinner at Nineteen18, one of the most prestigious restaurants in Vilnius. Offering farm-to-table fine dining with a seasonal focus, it's a fitting way to conclude your holiday adventure. Cap off the evening by watching the city's Christmas fireworks display, especially if your visit falls close to New Year's Eve.

Day 6: Departure Day

Morning: Enjoy a leisurely breakfast at your hotel or visit Backstage Café for some of the city's best coffee and pastries before heading to the airport. If you have time, visit the Church of St. Peter and St. Paul, famous for its intricate Baroque interior, before taking a taxi or bus back to Vilnius International Airport (VNO).

Pro Tips for First-Timers:

Book in Advance: Whether it's for your hotel or a Christmas concert, booking ahead is crucial during the festive season as Vilnius gets busier with visitors.

Dress Warmly: Lithuanian winters are cold, with temperatures often dropping below freezing. Layer up, and don't forget to bring good boots for walking on icy streets.

Try Local Foods: Make the most of your time by sampling traditional Lithuanian Christmas dishes such as kūčiukai and herring salad, which are integral to the holiday experience.

Get Around Easily: Vilnius has an excellent public transportation system, but many attractions are within walking distance if you stay near the Old Town.

This sample itinerary offers a balance of festive highlights, historical landmarks, and cultural immersion, ensuring that your Christmas vacation in Vilnius is both magical and memorable. Whether it's your first visit or a return trip, the city's holiday charm and warmth will leave a lasting impression.

Printed in Great Britain
by Amazon